Crossroads Career®
Work Book
7 steps to jobs, careers and God's calling

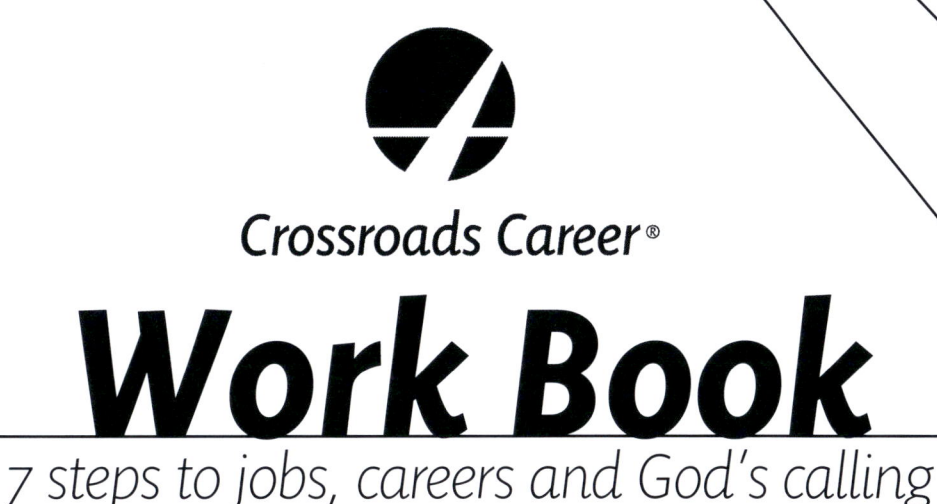

Your Name _____

Email _____

Phone _____

The Crossroads Career Work Book is a faith-based career and job search guide with exercises and devotionals. To order print copies or digital ebooks, please visit our online store at **www.crossroadscareer.org/workbook**. To gain access to all of the hot--links in this book, go to **www.crossroadscareer.org** and create an account.

Updated May 2014

Contents

For we are His workmanship, created in Christ Jesus for good works, which God prepared beforehand so that we would walk in them. EPHESIANS 2:10 NASB

step 1 upward **God's calling** 4
- Walk 7 steps through crossroads in your career
- Together everyone achieves more
- See progress every week

step 2 attitude **Reach forward** 15
- Practice 3 ways to improve your attitude
- Overcome anger, fear and depression
- Plan for your future and hope

step 3 aptitude **Discover your best** 22
- Learn 6 factors in your unique design
- Discover your gifts, passions and calling
- Find out what you do best

step 4 altitude **Target opportunities** 31
- Learn 6 factors to target opportunities
- Find people who need most what you do best
- Write resumes that get results

step 5 searching **Seek to serve** 42
- Learn 3 ways to effectively network
- Write your 30-second elevator pitch
- Seek and you shall find

step 6 sorting **Wow interviewers** 52
- Learn 4 steps for engaging interviews
- Practice interview questions
- Prepare for tests and references

step 7 selecting **Walk in good works** 62
- Learn to get, make and evaluate offers
- Seek win-win negotiation
- Get a new job jump start

congratulations! 69

step 1 - upward
Hear and Follow God's Calling

Stand at the Crossroads and Look

More than 150 million workers in the U.S. face crossroads in their careers every year. According to a recent Gallup® poll, 72% of them are actively disengaged or unengaged in their jobs. Are you one of them?

This is what the LORD says: "Stand at the crossroads and look; ask for the ancient paths, ask where the good way is, and walk in it, and you will find rest for your souls..." JEREMIAH 6:16

We teach a 7-step process that helps people to hear and follow God's calling, as they explore careers and search for the right job. Over 30,000 people have connected with us looking for help. The first step we recommend is to look upward.

Upward – Inward – Outward

"You shall love the Lord your God with all your heart and with all your soul and with all your mind. This is the great and first commandment. And a second is like it: You shall love your neighbor as yourself. On these two commandments depend all the Law and the Prophets." Matthew 22:37-40.

Ken Boa in his book *Face to Face* sums it up this way:

Love God completely – **Upward**
Love yourself correctly – **Inward**
Love others compassionately – **Outward**

Because God loves you, you can love Him. You can begin to see yourself through His eyes, as His masterpiece created for good works. When you love yourself correctly, then you are free to love others compassionately. All of a sudden you are not just looking for a job or career. You are learning to seek and serve others who need most what you do best.

Now is your opportunity to learn how to make the most of every moment.

Imagine realizing your gifts, passions and calling at work. Think of yourself as an explorer – ready for adventure.

Therefore be careful how you walk, not as unwise men but as wise, making the most of your time... EPHESIANS 5:15-16 NASB

You are not too young, not too old. It is not too late. You are not stuck in muck. You can survive and thrive. Career crossing opportunities bring out the best in you and the best for you:

- Discover new abilities and passions.
- Find different jobs and careers where your strengths bring greater value.
- Meet new people. Make new friends as you find help, hope and fellowship.
- Count your blessings, reprioritize what is important and recommit yourself.
- Draw nearer to God and His plans.

Job Satisfaction: Fulfilling & Fruitful?

A 2011 survey of U.S. households conducted for The Conference Board by Nielsen, finds that only 47.2% of Americans are satisfied with their jobs. How about you?

Put a check mark beside each descriptor that applies to you:

Unemployed because ...
- ☐ Quit, laid off or fired
- ☐ Nearly or newly graduated from college or high school
- ☐ Recently divorced or going back to work after raising children
- ☐ Relocated or relocating and seeking new job
- ☐ Coming out of retirement

Misemployed, miserable, unengaged or nervous because ...
- ☐ St-st-st-stress!
- ☐ Worried about losing your job
- ☐ Actively disengaged in your job
- ☐ Unengaged, bored and/or in a rut
- ☐ Need or want to work from home
- ☐ Working for a boss behaving badly
- ☐ Just do not like or not good at what you are doing
- ☐ Not enough money - too many hours - maybe both
- ☐ Want to be an independent contractor or maybe own a business
- ☐ Spending too much time "on the road again" either commuting or traveling
- ☐ You relate to the song "16 tons" by Merle Travis...

"You load 16 tons, and what do you get? Another day older and deeper in debt. Saint Peter don't call me 'cause I can't go. I owe my soul to the company store."

Happily employed, but ...
- ☐ Successful and prosperous, but lacking a sense of greater purpose, vision and mission
- ☐ Half-way through your life and wondering about the "second half"
- ☐ Vanity of vanities! All is vanity.
  ECCLESIASTES 1:2 NASB

Fulfilled and called ...
- ☐ Loving Mondays – passionate about the work you do
- ☐ Using God-given abilities, interests, personality and values
- ☐ Living and working with a sense of purpose, mission and fulfillment
- ☐ Hearing and following God's calling and maximizing you career

Circle the words on the range of work situations that best describe how you feel now ...

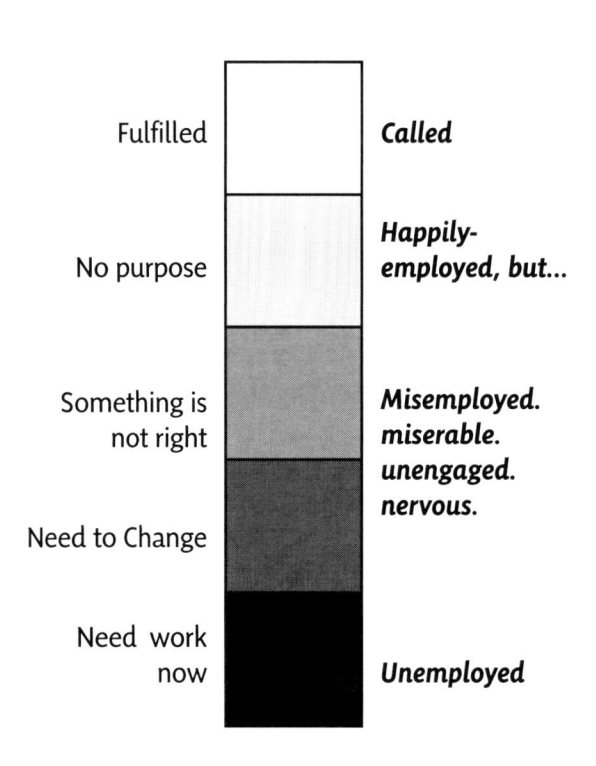

Fulfilled	**Called**
No purpose	**Happily-employed, but...**
Something is not right	**Misemployed. miserable. unengaged. nervous.**
Need to Change	
Need work now	**Unemployed**

Do What You Do Best

Do you have the opportunity to do what you do best every day at work? For most of us, the answer is unfortunately "No!"

In the United States, "the majority of American adults say they are not able to use their strengths to do what they do best throughout the day" according to 2012 Gallup® research.

You are God's unique masterpiece created for good works. How different would your work life be if you could do what you do and like best every day? You would be happier and more productive.

Discover your gifts (experiences, abilities and personality) and your passions (what you like and value).

Look for opportunities with your current employer to offer your best. One major corporation's career development program found that:

- 30% of their employees were in the right jobs.
- 55% of their employees were in the wrong jobs and better fits for other jobs in the company.
- 15% left the company.

Don't wait. Take charge of yourself and your career. Discover your best, and target new opportunities.

Make Bad Work Better

If you are anything less than fulfilled and fruitful in your work, you might be contributing to the problem without even realizing it. If you are doing anything less than your very best in your work, you are short-changing yourself, your employer and God.

If you have a bad attitude about your work, your boss, your co-workers or any other aspect of your work, that attitude will effect your performance and relationships.

To maximize your career in your current job, consider this:

Does this describe you and how you work?
_____

Whatever you do, work at it with all your heart, as working for the Lord, not for men, since you know that you will receive an inheritance from the Lord as a reward. It is the Lord Christ you are serving.
COLOSSIANS 3:22-24

Are you working heartily and with sincerity of heart? Are you serving God in your job? Maybe you are thinking, "Yeah, but you don't know my boss." You're right, but consider this:
_____

… submit yourselves to your masters with all respect, not only to those who are good and considerate, but also to those who are harsh.
1 PETER 2:18

If "harsh" describes your boss, it is especially important to take your attitude and performance to their highest. One way to improve your attitude and work performance is to visit **Character First** at **www.characterfirst.com/aboutus/qualities**. You may discover your situation changes for the better, when you have change how you are working.

Crossroads in your Career

The Crossroads Career process consists of walking through 7 steps:

step 1 - upward	**God's Calling**
step 2 - attitude	**Reach Forward**
step 3 - aptitude	**Discover Your Best**
step 4 - altitude	**Target Opportunities**
step 5 - searching	**Seek to Serve**
step 6 - sorting	**Wow Interviewers**
step 7 - selecting	**Walk in Good Works**

Notice in the diagram below that Upward is first and foremost. Attitude and Aptitude provide movement and direction that give your career Altitude, which then leads to Searching, Sorting and Selecting.

Step 1 is God's calling. Steps 2-3-4 are planning the work. The last three steps are working the plan.

```
        2 attitude
        Reach Forward

7 selecting                3 aptitude
Walk in Good Works         Discover your Best

        1 upward
        God's Calling

6 sorting                  4 altitude
Wow Interviewers           Target Opportunities

        5 searching
        Seek to Serve
```

If you are actively searching for a new job, you are probably focused on steps 5 and 6. If you are exploring a career change, you might be more focused on steps 3 and 4. If you search for a very long time, you may experience walking from steps 1 through 7, and then have to go all the way back to step 1. You will find it helpful to know every week where you are and what is next. Review earlier steps and make changes in what you are doing based on what you have learned so far.

Write down the step you are in right now: _____ .

Hear and Follow God's Calling

How great would it be to hear and follow the upward call of God? Imagine getting up every day with the conviction that you are on the planet for a purpose. How fulfilled would you be to know that you and your work matter to God and that He is pleased? But how, you ask? Read through, consider and exercise 11 ways to hear and follow God's calling.

---

1. <u>Worship</u> God

There is no calling without a Caller. Take dedicated time to worship, glorify, praise and thank Him. Then as you live and work every day from waking until sleeping, do everything to honor Him.

Ascribe to the LORD the glory due his name; worship ... in the splendor of his holiness.
PSALM 29:2

2. Read and Study the <u>Bible</u>

The Bible is God's authority and our manual for living. Consider it as bread, and feed from it every day. If you have never read the Bible, consider starting with the book of John, Ephesians or Psalms.

Your word is a lamp to my feet and a light for my path.
PSALM 119:105

3. <u>Pray</u>

Be in conversation with God every day, perhaps multiple times during every day. He is always available. Pray for guidance. Read a Psalm as your own personal prayer.

Show me the way I should go, for to you I lift up my soul. PSALM 143:8

4. <u>Listen</u> to God

Prayer is two-way communication. In a journal, notebook or this Work Book, write thoughts that come to your mind for later reflection and Bible study.

Be still, and know that I am God. PSALM 46:10

5. Be with <u>Christians</u>

Spend time with Christians you like and who like you. Study the Bible together. Pray together. Encourage one another. Follow the ABCs of Accountability, Belonging and Care.

...consider how we may spur one another on toward love and good deeds. HEBREWS 10:24

6. Seek Wise <u>Counsel</u>

Seek wisdom first from above (James 3:17) and then from other people. Some may be friends. Some may be strangers with whom we talk only once.

Let the wise listen and add to their learning, and let the discerning get guidance. PROVERBS 1:5

Crossroads Career® Work Book © Copyright 2000-2013 Crossroads Career Services, Inc. All rights reserved.

7. Consider **Circumstances**

Be a good steward of the opportunities God gives you. Consider each situation with God in prayer. Always measure your prayer, counsel and unfolding circumstances in light of the truth of the Bible.

Be very careful, then, how you live ...making the most of every opportunity... EPHESIANS 5:15-16

8. **Confess** and Clear Your Head

A clear head is critical in thinking through options and seeking God's leading. It is easy to become confused, especially if sin is getting in the way. Confess it, and clear it out every day.

If we confess our sins, He is faithful and righteous to forgive us our sins and to cleanse us...
1 JOHN 1:9 NASB

9. Be Alert for God's **Peace**

As you consider various options and paths, be alert for the peace that transcends all understanding, even in the midst of the most chaotic of times.

And the peace of God, which transcends all understanding, will guard your hearts and your minds in Christ Jesus. PHILIPPIANS 4:7

10. Keep a **Journal**

Keep track of what you learn from your Bible reading, thoughts you have during prayer, advice you receive from your friends, unfolding circumstances, and things that bring you God's peace.

Thus says the LORD ... "Write all the words which I have spoken to you in a book." JEREMIAH 30:2 NASB

11. **Trust** and Obey

There is no other way! If you think the Lord wants you to do something, and it seems to be in alignment with everything we have been talking about, then do it! If you hear Him, follow Him.

"Whoever has my commands and obeys them, he is the one who loves me. He who loves me will be loved by my Father, and I too will love him and show myself to him." JOHN 14:21

God is Calling You

Good news! God, who created the world and everything in it, wants to have a personal relationship with you. He made it possible by His Son paying the price for your sin, the only thing that separates you from Him. By accepting His Son as payment on your behalf, you can have a relationship with the Creator of the universe, starting now and for eternity.

For God so loved the world, that He gave His only begotten Son, that whoever believes in Him shall not perish, but have eternal life. JOHN 3:16 NASB

Even in the midst of the agony of defeat, it is possible to experience victory. You can discover that God is good. God is great. Seek Him and His righteousness, and all the other things He has prepared will be added to you. Work out your faith in Him upward, inward and outward. He made you for good works.

Read & Write Devotional

Career + Calling = Maximize Your Career

Career, according to *dictionary.com*, means "an occupation or profession, especially one requiring special training, followed as one's lifework: *He sought a career as a lawyer.*"

Calling comes from the Greek KALEO, which means "to call anyone, invite, summon." It refers primarily to a divine call as it relates to a vocation or redemption.

Based on the definitions above, what are the differences between career and calling? Write your thoughts about the differences below.

Career	Calling

Pray for God to enlighten the eyes of your heart so you may know the hope of His calling.

I pray also that the eyes of [my] heart may be enlightened
in order that [I] may know the hope to which he has called [me],
the riches of his glorious inheritance in the saints,
and his incomparably great power for us who believe.
That power is like the working of his mighty strength. EPHESIANS 1:18-19

Invest in You

You are your most important asset. Be a good steward of yourself. Invest time, money and effort in you.

Time

If you are unemployed, invest 40 hours a week. If you are employed, invest 7 hours a week. Smart planning and weekly commitment are required. Finding the right work is hard work that takes time!

- **How long to find work?** That is a tough question to answer, because it depends on your sense of urgency, how many hours you invest, what you are looking for, your search plan and how well you execute it. The U.S. Bureau of Labor Statistics reported in 2011 that the length of unemployment averaged over 6 months! For updated reports go to **www.bls.gov/cps**.

- **How long to change careers?** It may take a few weeks to a few years. The more education and experience you need to change careers, the longer it will take. The key is to start now by discovering your strengths and targeting occupations and industries that need them most.

Money

In light of how much money you want to make, answer the question, "How much am I willing to invest?" Set a budget and consider including these potential expenses.

	ESTIMATED INVESTMENT
Additional education, skills training, certifications, degrees	$ _____
Career books, directories, publications or web services	$ _____
Career assessments and perhaps hire a professional coach	$ _____
Trade and professional association memberships and meetings	$ _____
Extra phone, phone lines and charges; email & Internet access	$ _____
Resumes, business cards and stationery; postage and shipping	$ _____
Local or perhaps long distance travel and meals	$ _____
New clothes and grooming	$ _____

Whatever amount you decide, set aside the money and invest it wisely. Keep good records. Costs related to a job search may qualify as tax deductions. Check with the IRS, your tax preparer or an accountant.

Effort

This Work Book will work for you if you work hard at it. Read every page. Complete every exercise. Read and write every devotional. When you find tough areas, ask for help, encouragement and support.

Plan your activities and make progress every week using **SMART** goals.

Specific: Set goals that are measurable. Define exactly what you want to accomplish.

Moderate: Select 2-5 goals per week. Too many goals can be overwhelming.

Accountability: Show and tell somebody what you plan to do, and let them know how you did.

Record: It is helpful and motivating to keep a written record of your goals and progress.

Time-activated: Put in your calendar goals by days and times during the week.

Weekly Progress Review & Preview Exercise

For This Coming Week of _____

Power your career every week Sunday through Saturday with SMART goals.

Specific: Set goals that are measurable. Define exactly what you want to accomplish.
Moderate: Select 2-5 goals per week. Too many goals can be overwhelming.
Accountability: Show and tell somebody what you plan to do, and let them know how you did.
Record: It is helpful and motivating to keep a written record of your goals and progress.
Time-activated: Put in your calendar goals by days and times during the week.

High point of last week:		Low point of last week:	

Celebrate progress from last week

1.
2.
3.
4.
5.

Things learned that could be useful

Set SMART goals for this coming week

1.
2.
3.
4.
5.

What help is needed most?

TEAM:
Together Everyone Achieves More

Most people find that the more connections they make, the merrier it is for everyone.

... let us consider how to stimulate one another to love and good deeds, not forsaking our own assembling together, as is the habit of some, but encouraging one another. HEBREWS 10:24-25 NASB

Some of the most popular environments are small groups for either support or study, workshops and network meetings where you meet other career explorers, learn job search skills, get ideas and find referrals to others. It is best to meet once a week at a regular time and place.

See if there is a Crossroads Career group near you at **www.crossroadscareer.org**. Also look for opportunities to connect with others through local business and professional networking groups; colleges and universities; job and career fairs; career and job placement centers – especially those sponsored by department of labor career centers which you can find through **www.servicelocator.org**. To start a job club, study group or career ministry in your church or community, school or college, coaching or counseling practice, check out **www.crossroadscareer.org/groups**.

Meet with Others... It's Better Together!

Using the Crossroads Career Work Book in a small group study, in workshops or with a friend/mentor/coach is better than studying alone. The accountability, belonging and care with others multiplies your strength and wisdom. Here are tips for meeting with others:

1. Attend all the meetings.
2. Do all your homework before meetings.
3. Bring this Work Book and a Bible to every meeting.
4. Stay in touch with others between meetings by email or phone.
5. Arrive early and plan to stay until it is over to take advantage of networking time.
6. Please pay attention to the facilitator(s), as well as to your fellow teammates.
7. If you have questions, concerns or critiques, please share them with your facilitator(s).
8. Maintain confidentiality. What is said in the group should stay in the group.

DAY OF WEEK: _____ TIME FROM _____ TO _____

ADDRESS: _____

FACILITATOR: _____ PHONE: _____ EMAIL: _____

Get Career Dashboard and Resources for Free!
www.crossroadscareer.org

The benefits of registering online are:

- Login to your own career dashboard where you save resumes, cover letters, job searches. Get prayer portal, daily career tips, scriptures and over 200 career and job search resources.

- Download and save the Work Book on your computer to use online. It is filled with hotlinks that you can click and instantly go to helpful websites, career tools, articles and more.

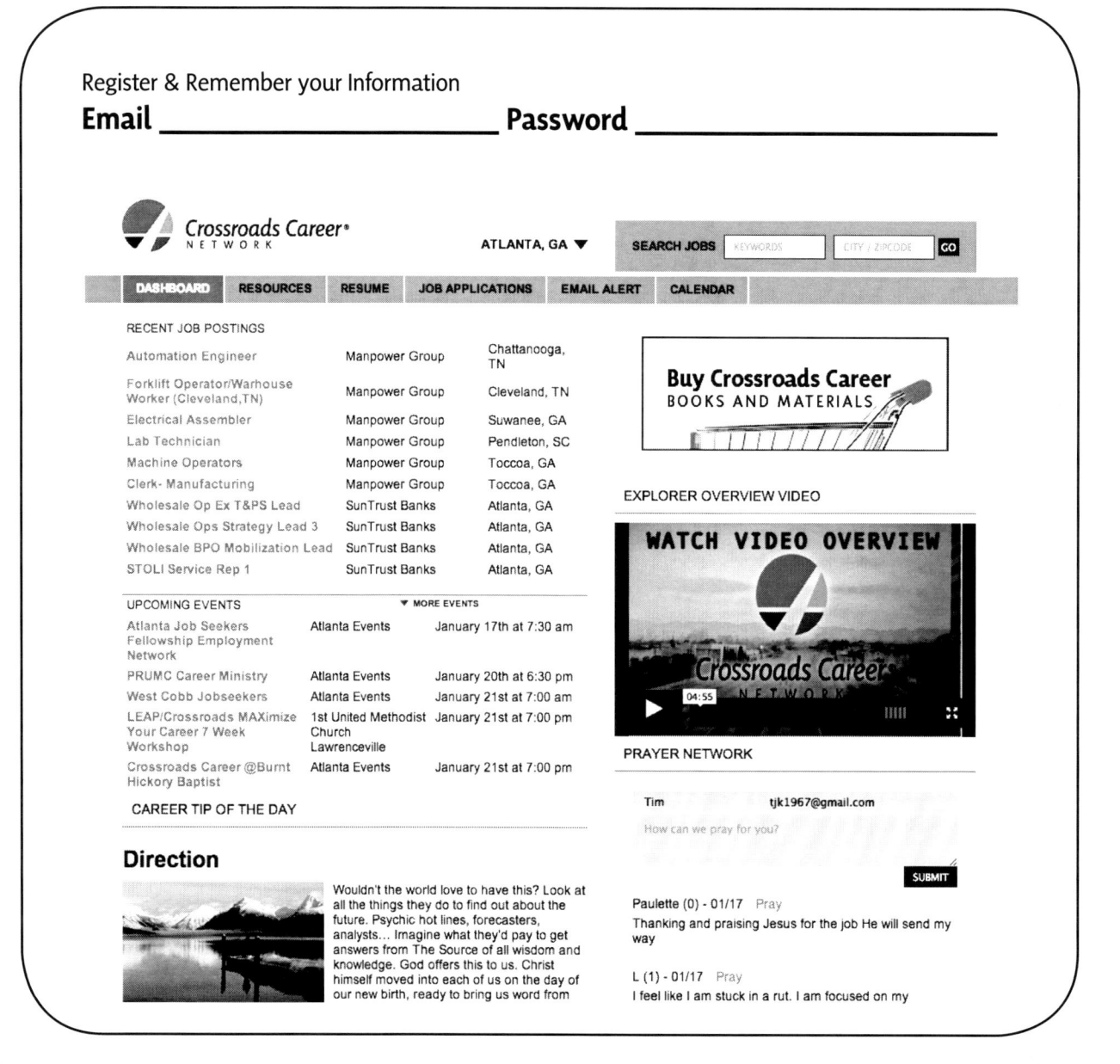

Register & Remember your Information

Email _____ **Password** _____

step 2 - attitude
Reach Forward

Consider It Pure Joy

Most people enter a crossroads with a mixture of positive and negative feelings.

Unemployed? Are you angry, fearful, and depressed or relieved with renewed energy.

Misemployed? Is your work miserable or are you filled with hope for something new.

Are you **happily-employed**, but you feel empty, or are you seeking purpose.

As you think, so you shall be. Consider...

"85% of the reason people get jobs and get ahead in those jobs is because of attitude," Zig Ziglar, author of *Over the Top*.

"Most folks are about as happy as they make up their minds to be" Abraham Lincoln, 16th President of the United States.

Consider it pure joy, my brothers, when you face trials of many kinds, because you know that the testing of your faith develops perseverance. Perseverance must finish its work. JAMES 1:2-4

Where do you rank on the 10-point Attitude-O-Meter?

ATTITUDE-O-METER   BRIEFLY DESCRIBE YOUR CIRCUMSTANCES

Joy	Good
10	
9	
8	
7	Bad
6	
5	
4	
3	
2	Ugly
1	
0	
The Pit	

Does your attitude reflect your circumstances? Bad situations breed bad feelings. A positive attitude turns stumbling blocks into building blocks. You feel better, and you think better.

Is it possible to be in The Pit circumstantially, yet live each day with joy? "Impossible" you say? All things are "HimPossible" to those who live upward, inward and outward. Start with a decision to reset your attitude. Go back to the Attitude-O-Meter and draw a square around a higher number.

Congratulations! You have just begun working toward a new, more positive and joyful attitude. Now let's look at the work required to reach this new attitude setting.

Build a Positive Attitude

Discover the three principles for building a positive attitude

1. "Forgetting what lies behind" is about accepting loss.
2. "Reaching forward to what lies ahead" is about accepting opportunity.
3. "Pressing toward the goal of the prize of the upward call of God" requires strength training.

...forgetting what lies behind and reaching forward to what lies ahead, I press on toward the goal for the prize of the upward call of God in Christ Jesus. PHILIPPIANS 3:13-14 NASB

Forget What Lies Behind

"Forgetting what lies behind" means accepting the loss of something you either had or had hoped for. Whether you lost your job, or you are in a job that you wish you *could* lose, you will find freedom to move to the future if you admit, understand and grieve the loss, no matter how minor or major it may be.

You can expect to experience one or more of the following feelings at some level of intensity--maybe a little, maybe a lot. As you admit your feelings about your situation, you may feel that you have been used, abused and refused. Maybe you are blaming others; your boss, a coworker, someone else – maybe even yourself.

Do you ever hear yourself making any of these statements?

To help you process, write about your situation and your feelings in a private journal. You can talk about it with people you trust, people who care about you: your spouse, a parent, a sibling, a friend or business associate, someone from church, a minister or a counselor.

The real key to overcoming anger, however, is to exercise forgiveness toward everyone involved – not for their benefit – but for yours. As you write or talk about your situation, visualize every person you are blaming, and make a conscious decision to begin forgiving each one every day.

Let go of the past, so the past can let go of you. Only then can you reach toward the future. Go to the next page now and work through the exercise "Anger is One Letter Short of Danger."

Do not let the sun go down on your anger. EPHESIANS 4:26 NASB

Whenever you stand praying, forgive, if you have anything against anyone, so that your Father who is in heaven will also forgive you your transgressions." MARK 11:25 NASB

STATEMENTS	FEELINGS
This can't be. I don't believe it!	Denial <-> Shock
What do I do? How do I handle this?	Distraction <-> Panic
They can't do that to me! I will get them!	Irritation <-> Anger
I'm tired and don't feel like doing anything.	Feeling Down <-> Depression
I don't feel well/headache/stomachache!	Stress <-> Physical Illness

Exercise

"Anger" is One Letter Short of "Danger"

When you see red, it is an alarm that "Danger Is Ahead!" Everyone feels anger sometimes. It is what you do with your anger that counts. Use these steps below to help you forgive yourself and others, let go of your anger, and put the past behind you.

1. Describe the offense and how you feel about it.
2. List everyone you blame (this list may include yourself).

Describe the Offense - The Specific Action(s) that Caused the Anger	How You Feel About the Offense	First Names of "Offenders"	Now Forgive Each Person Involved

3. Forgive! One key to being able to forgive is recognizing how much God, your Heavenly Father, has forgiven you. Every time you feel anger or bitterness, ask God to help you forgive. You may find the following prayer helpful.

> *"Heavenly Father, thank you for the riches of Your kindness, forbearance and patience, knowing that Your kindness has led me to repentance (Romans 2:4). I confess that I have not extended that same patience and kindness towards others who have offended me, but instead I have harbored bitterness and resentment. I pray that during this time of self-examination, You would bring to mind only those people that I have not forgiven in order that I may do so (Matthew 18:35). I also pray that if I have offended others, You would bring to mind only those people from whom I need to seek forgiveness and the extent to which I need to seek it (Matthew 5:23-24). I ask this in the name of Jesus."*
>
> **THE BONDAGE BREAKER, BY NEIL T. ANDERSON**

Reach Forward to What Lies Ahead

"Reaching forward" is about overcoming fear and accepting the opportunity that awaits you – both in depth and breadth.

In Depth

This is the first day of the rest of your life. You can make decisions now for the better that will last forever. Ask yourself:

- How would I like to see my future?
- Am I on the planet for a purpose?
- When I am 84 years old looking back on my life, what would I like to see?
- How will God view my life?

See a future for yourself in which you are maximizing your full career potential. Begin to picture your work and calling in ways in which you are content, fulfilled and in alignment with God's will. Make plans and think about what it will take to accomplish them one step at a time.

"For I know the plans I have for you," declares the LORD, "plans to prosper you and not to harm you, plans to give you hope and a future." JEREMIAH 29:11

In Breadth

There are more than 100 major industry groups, each one with thousands of employers. There are more than 960 major occupations with millions of workers.

Whole industries and occupations come and go – sometimes rapidly. Millions more people are becoming self-employed versus employer-employed. You can no longer rely on an employer to guide your career. It is up to you to find your own way. Part of your work is to learn how to find work. You have to figure out what you do and like best, and then find an employer or customer who needs and wants it most.

The market for workers is global. Imagine an independent contractor in North Carolina working for an office in China, owned by a British company doing business in Iraq.

Opportunities abound! You might be asking: "Where are they?" and "How do I get them?"

That is the reason for this Work Book. Steps 3 and 4 of our 7-step process will help you discover your best and target opportunities. Steps 5, 6 and 7 will help you find and get the best opportunity for you.

Yet, fear of the unknown can be a factor. Go to the next page and work through the exercise "Face the Fear."

Be anxious for nothing, but in everything by prayer and supplication with thanksgiving, let your requests be made known to God. And the peace of God, which surpasses all comprehension, shall guard your hearts and your minds in Christ Jesus. PHILIPPIANS 4:6-7 NASB

Exercise

Face the Fear

1. List people, places, things and activities that make you anxious about career transition.
2. Following the principle that "perfect love casts out fear," do what would be in the best interest of people involved. Pray for and help people who make you anxious. Trust God to work out the details.

People, Places, Things and Activities You Fear in Job/Career Search	Specific Actions for Moving through Your Fears

3. Think of people who can encourage and pray for you; people you trust, people who care about you – your spouse, a parent, a sibling, a friend or business associate, someone from church, a minister or a counselor. Ask them to pray for you, and write their names here:

_____
_____
_____

4. When anxiety appears as a companion to your day, greet it with this prayer:

> "In the name and by the authority of the Lord Jesus Christ, I bind all lying spirits causing fear and anxiety in me. God has not given us a spirit of fear and timidity, but of power, love and a sound mind/discipline. (2 Timothy 1:7). I therefore reject all fear and choose to walk by faith in the Holy Spirit's power, live in the light of God's love, and think with the sound mind of Christ."
>
> FREEDOM FROM FEAR, BY NEIL T. ANDERSON

Press on Toward the Goal

"Pressing on" requires personal strength training, which creates much needed energy and endurance. You will need to build your strength for the journey ahead – and with strength comes courage. Consider this formula for a personal strength training exercise program. **Eat right, exercise and get plenty of rest:**

Physically

Pay attention to nutrition; cut calories and fat; reduce caffeine and alcohol. Exercise 3-5 times a week, if a doctor approves. Get at least 7 hours of sleep a night.

Mentally

Feed your mind good thoughts. Spend time with good friends. Do things you enjoy. Be sure to spend some time alone to rejuvenate. Do nothing and give your brain a break.

Spiritually

Spend time alone with God every day by praying and reading the Bible. Start with 10 minutes, then go to 20 minutes or more. Get together with others for Bible study, prayer and fellowship.

Get Help for Other Pressure Points

Financial stress can turn a difficult situation really sour. Two ways to alleviate financial pressure are to earn more and spend less. Since you have more control over spending than earning, look at your spending habits and financial obligations. If you don't have a budget, create one, especially in light of understanding the income and benefits needed from a job (see page 64). If you have debt, add it up and pay it down. The less income you need, the more freedom you have to accept the right job for you.

- Compass-finances God's way
  www.compass1.org
- Crown Financial Ministries
  www.crown.org
- Financial Peace University
  www.daveramsey.com/fpu

Family problems might get worse in the midst of a career crossroads, but they can also improve! Husbands and wives have opportunities to love, respect and support one another. Communication, collaboration and commitment are critical components to working together. Do not withdraw, but rather stay connected not only to each other, but also to family, friends and church. For more help, contact:

- Focus on the Family: **www.family.org**.

Personal issues can be faced better with someone with whom you can talk. Find a person who cares about you, who you trust, who has no vested interest in what you decide, and who seems to have competency to help: your church pastor or care ministry, your best friend or a professional counselor. Be careful about forming friendships with the opposite gender outside of your marriage. For more help, contact:

- American Association of Christian Counselors at **www.aacc.net** for an online directory.

As you press on toward the goal, remember the ultimate source of help and strength …

But those who hope in the LORD will renew their strength. They will soar on wings like eagles; they will run and not grow weary; they will walk and not be faint. ISAIAH 40:31

Read & Write Devotional

Your Hope & Future

"For I know the plans I have for you," declares the LORD, "plans to prosper you and not to harm you, plans to give you hope and a future." JEREMIAH 29:11

See a future for yourself in which you are not only maximizing your career, but you are experiencing an overall sense of wellbeing. Consider goals for your whole life …

- Career Work Life
- Community
- Social, Family & Friends
- Physical & Health
- Financial
- **?**

We have met people who climbed the ladder of success, only to find it leaning against the wrong wall. The question mark in the diagram represents the purpose of your goals, which helps you set goals worth getting. Ask God to give you a peek at your future as you think about your purpose and goals.

What thoughts come to your mind? Write them down here.

If you are interested to know more about your wellbeing, go to **www.wbfinder.com**

step 3 - aptitude
Discover Your Best

There is no one like you anywhere. Never has been. Never will be. You are uniquely designed by God. No other person on the planet has your DNA and personal history.

For You (God) created my inmost being; you knit me together in my mother's womb. I praise you because I am fearfully and wonderfully made... PSALM 139:13-14

5 Factors In Your Unique Design

The better you understand you, the better you can see how to maximize your career. Most professionals in career planning and recruiting consider 5 factors:

1. Experiences – Your background – Personal, educational, vocational

2. Abilities – What you do best – Talents, knowledge, skills

3. Personality – How you do best what you do – Natural behavior traits

4. Interests – What you like most – People, places, things and activities you enjoy

5. Values – What is important to you – Work and life purpose, principles or burdens

Experiences+Abilities+Personality = Gifts:
Your gifts are the combination of your experiences, abilities (talents, knowledge, skills), and your personality (natural behavioral traits).

Interests+Values = Passions:
Your passions include your interests (what you like best) and your values (what is important to you). Passions motivate you to use your gifts in particular ways and places.

Employ Passions, As Well As Gifts

"A team of researchers followed a group of 1,500 people over a period of 20 years. At the outset of the study, the participants were divided into 2 groups:

- Group A, 83% of the sample, was composed of people embarking on a career path they had chosen solely for the prospect of making money now in order to do what they wanted later in life.
- Group B, the other 17% of the sample, consisted of people who had chosen their career paths so that they could do what they wanted now and worry about the money later.

"The data showed some startling revelations:
- At the end of the 20-year period, 101 of the 1,500 had become millionaires.
- Of the millionaires, all but one - 100 out of 101 - were from Group B, the group that had chosen to pursue what they loved.

"The key ingredient in most successful projects is loving what you do. Having a goal or a plan is not enough. Academic preparation is not enough. Prior experience is not enough. Enjoyment of your life's work is the key," explain Robert J. Kriegel & Louis Patler in *If It Ain't Broke... BREAK IT!*

Introducing the "X" Factor

The "X" Factor is the active presence of Jesus Christ in your life, including your work. It begins the millisecond you are created anew in Christ Jesus by accepting Him as your Lord and Savior.

Therefore if anyone is in Christ, he is a new creature; the old things passed away; behold, new things have come.
2 CORINTHIANS 5:17 NASB

Your gifts and passions, ignited by the Holy Spirit, are manifested as spiritual gifts and God's calling for you to minister for the good of others, not only in church, but also in your home and work life.

Discover Your Best

To get a well-rounded view of your strengths, we recommend 4 steps:

1. **Self-Assessments:** Think of these exercises as interviewing yourself. Complete all 3 Exercises on pages 24-26 to inventory your experiences, accomplishments and keywords.
2. **Ask Others Assessments:** Ask people from work, school, family and friends about your experience, accomplishments, abilities, values, interests and personality. See exercise on page 27.
3. **Professional Assessments:** We recommend three professional online assessments to give you more insight into you: PLACE, Career Direct® and StrengthsFinder® assessments. For more information and instructions, go to page 28.
4. **Summarize** what you do best. Enter keywords in Read & Write Devotional on page 29.

If you are registered on the Crossroads Career website, you can login to download, save and print multiple copies of the Self-Assessment, "Ask Others and Summarize Exercises" from Resources under Step 2.

Develop Your Best

You have natural strengths and weaknesses.

Once upon a time, training focused on everyone being good at everything, which meant that you worked extra hard trying to make your natural weaknesses stronger. The problem was no matter how much training you got, if you were not talented in a particular area, you would never be great!

Today, more attention is being paid to identifying your talents – your most natural thoughts, feelings and behaviors. Your talents are foundational and reflected in your personality, interests, values, spiritual gifts and calling.

Add knowledge and skills to your talents to build and become your personal best.

**Self-Assessment
Experiences Exercise**

Count Your Blessings

List places you worked and work you did from high school to the present. Make sure to include work for which you were paid and major volunteer work, educational projects, internships and extracurricular activities. Circle the places and the work that you did best and liked most.

Work you did	Places you worked
OCCUPATIONS: *Positions held, jobs, titles* EXAMPLES: *Teacher, sales manager, stock clerk*	INDUSTRIES: *Employers, organizations, customers* EXAMPLES: *Grocery store, school, military, church*

Aptitude / Crossroads Career

Self-Assessment
Accomplishments Exercise

You are a STAR

Think of as many accomplishments as you can, and describe them with this 4-step process.

1. What **Situation** did you face?
2. What was the **Task** to be accomplished?
3. What **Actions** did you take?
4. What **Results** did you achieve?

Each accomplishment you describe becomes a story about you as a STAR candidate, which helps you discover what you do best, target opportunities, write resumes, network and interview successfully.

ACCOMPLISHMENT EXAMPLE: Turned around sales in a newly-assigned territory

Situation You Faced	Tasks to Accomplish	Actions You Took	Results Acheived
Assigned new territory where sales had declined by 18% the prior year.	Increase sales 10% by end of the year.	Surveyed customers about satisfaction. Identified new competitor with cheaper product. Put on seminar for past, current and prospective customers featuring service.	Regained 63% of past customers, added 27 new customers, and increased sales 24%.

ACCOMPLISHMENT: _____

Self-Assessment Keywords Exercise

You are an A+ VIP

You are an A+VIP. Prayerfully review your experience and accomplishment self-assessments from pages 24 and 25. Write keywords to describe your Abilities, Values, Interests, and Personality.

Abilities
What you do best: talents, knowledge, skills

Values
What is important to you: purpose, principles, burdens

Interests
What you like most: people, places, things, activities

Personality
How you do best what you do: natural behavioral traits

Exercise

Ask Others Assessment

Ask for input from people who know you well: Work associates and supervisors, teachers, customers, vendors, volunteers, friends and family members.

Instructions to the Person Completing This Form: Thank you for taking the time to answer a few questions. Please share what you know about the person who gave you this form. Details are important, and specific examples can be helpful. Feel free to use the back of the form for extra space. Please be open and honest.

Accomplishments How would you describe their biggest accomplishments?

Abilities What do they do well? What are their talents, knowledge and skills.

Interests What do they like best? What people, places, things and activities do they enjoy most?

Personality What positive personality traits come to mind when you think of this person?

Values What positive values and character strengths does this person have?

Blind Spots / Weaknesses What improvements does this person need to make?

"Perfect" Career Fit What job or career do you think would be perfect for this person?

Exercise

Professional Assessments

We recommend and provide you access to 3 professional online assessments.

1. Find Your Place in Life

PLACE is a Bible-based, self-discovery process that helps you realize your ideal PLACE in life, work and ministry. This 5-step process guides you in developing your profile that includes:

P = Personality Discovery

L = Learning Spiritual Gifts

A = Abilities Awareness

C = Connecting Passion with Ministry

E = Experiences in Life

It is a great assessment for a quick summary. It takes less than an hour, and your reports are instantly available. Take it now online at **www.crossroadscareer.org/place**.

2. You've Got Talents

Everyone – including you – has talents. Based on a 40-year study of human strengths, the Gallup® organization created a language of the 34 most common talents and developed the Clifton StrengthsFinder® assessment to help people discover and describe these talents. You can discover your top 5 talent themes to which you can add knowledge and skills to develop your strengths. Over a million people have taken it.

Learn more at
www.gallupstrengthscenter.com/purchase

3. Career Direct® GE Assessment and Consultation

Explore your potential to be more, do more, and miximize your God-given abilities. This personal growth resource system is based on biblical principles of work to help you find your God-given design and steward your talents well. It starts with a unique online assessment followed by a personal consultation:

- Takes about an hour to complete. Reports are instantly available to your consultant.
- Analyzes four major career factors: personality, interest, skills and abilities, values
- Consultation includes an action Plan with high scoring career groups linked to the O*NET occupational database.
- Developed and improved for 20+ years.
- Exceeds statistical standards for validity and reliability.
- Provides clear direction to help make sound decisions in either of 2 applications:
  1. *Educational:* to find college and technical school majors that are best for you.
  2. *Occupational:* to help you discover your unique design and the assignment for your life.

Trained and certified consultants are ready to assist you through the process to help you understand your results. To learn more, visit **www.crossroadscareer.org/careerdirect**.

Exercise

Summarize Your Best

As each one has received a special gift, employ it in serving one another as good stewards of the manifold grace of God. 1 PETER 4:10 NASB

Do what you do best for people who need it most. You are a one-of-a-kind masterpiece with a unique mix of gifts, passions and calling. Explore all 6 factors to help you discover and develop your strengths:

Experiences – Your background – Personal, educational, vocational
Abilities – What you do best – Talents, knowledge, skills
Personality – How you do what you do best – Natural behavior traits
Interests – What you like best – People, places, things, activities you enjoy
Values – What is important to you – Work and life purpose, principles or points of pain
X Factor – What are your spiritual gifts – What is God's calling

Review all your exercises and assessment reports from pages 23-27. Look for common themes and keywords. Write the most important keywords in each of the following categories.

Gifts			Passions	
Experiences, Your Background	Abilities, Talents, Skills, Knowledge	Personality, Behavior Traits	Interests, What you Enjoy	Values, What's Important

X Factor Spiritual Gifts and Calling

Read & Write Devotional

You are God's Masterpiece

Do you think of yourself as God's masterpiece? Consider these two commandments...

"You shall love the Lord your God with all your heart and with all your soul and with all your mind. This is the great and first commandment. And a second is like it: You shall love your neighbor as yourself. On these two commandments depend all the Law and the Prophets." **Matthew 22:37-40.**

Did you skip over the part where it reads that you are supposed to love yourself? Here is what author Ken Boa in his book *Face to Face* writes about how you can love yourself...

"To love ourselves correctly is to see ourselves as God sees us and to allow the Word, not the world, to define who and whose we really are. The clearer we capture the vision of our new identity in Jesus Christ, the more we will realize that our deepest needs for security, significance and satisfaction are met in Him and not in people, possessions or positions."

**Take a few moments. Prayerfully reflect on pages 23-28.
See yourself as God sees you. Write your thoughts...**

_____
_____
_____
_____
_____
_____
_____
_____
_____
_____
_____
_____
_____
_____

step 4 - altitude
Target Opportunities

Attitude + Aptitude = Altitude which gives you the motivation and direction to do what you do best for people who need it most.

As each one has received a special gift, employ it in serving one another as good stewards of the manifold grace of God. 1 PETER 4:10 NASB

How to Target Opportunities

Listed below are 6 factors for targeting to think about and pray over:

1. **Occupations:** The work you do. Job functions you perform.
2. **Employers:** People and organizations for whom you work.
3. **Locations:** Where you work by city, state, country.
4. **Income:** How much you make in wages, salary and benefits.
5. **Platforms:** Employee, contractor, business owner, or volunteer.
6. **Culture:** Operating values that are important to you.

When you put these 6 targeting factors together, they look like a sighting scope…

```
        Occupations  |  Employers
        ─────── Opportunities ───────
        Locations    |  Income

             Platforms + Culture
```

Refer to the "Summarize Your Best" Exercise on page 29, as you use keywords to research the following 6 targeting factors.

1. Occupations: Explore occupations at **www.online.onetcenter.org/find**. Search using keywords and get lists with most relevant occupations. Click on the top 5 occupations to see work activities, abilities, interests, values, wages and employment. O*Net is the nation's primary source of information more than 960 occupations.

2. Employers: Research more than 100 major industry groups of employers. Each industry is described in terms of employment, trends, occupations and wages and more. Visit **www.bls.gov/iag**. For specific employers, start by searching **www.google.com**.

3. Locations: If you want to work near where you live now, use your home zip code with occupational or employer keywords in job boards and search engines to find prospective places hiring. If you want to relocate or explore other locations, go to **www.bestplaces.net**. You may want to search for cities with lower unemployment, which can mean more opportunities at higher pay; see **www.bls.gov/web/laummtrk.htm**. For exploring other countries, visit the CIA's World Fact Book at **www.cia.gov/library/publications**

4. Income: To find out how much jobs pay, go to **www.salary.com**. Income may consist of wages or salary, commissions, bonuses or tips; benefits such as insurance and retirement plans; etc. For a helpful checklist, see "Understanding the Offer" Exercise on page 64. It is best to be as flexible as possible by reducing your cost of living as much as you can, especially if you are changing careers during which time you may earn less as you learn a new occupation or industry.

5. Platforms: Employee, contractor, owner, or volunteer. In the new world of work, it is wise to be flexible and open to four different working platforms.

EMPLOYEE: You are an employee *if the employer can control what will be done and how it will be done*. Employers must withhold income, Social Security and Medicare taxes. At the end of the calendar year, employers issue W-2 statements to employees about earnings and taxes withheld. Advantages include:
- Qualifying for company benefits such as medical insurance and savings or retirement benefits
- Receiving training, development and other career-enhancing benefits
- Being counted as part of the organization

SELF-EMPLOYED CONTRACTOR: If you are a contractor, employers have the right to control or direct only the result of the work done by a contractor, but not the means and methods of accomplishing the result. Employers do not withhold taxes on payments to contractors. At the end of the year, employers issue 1099 statements that summarize earnings. It is the responsibility of the contractor to file estimated tax payments to the IRS, as well as file annual taxes. Advantages include:
- Higher rates of pay for a particular job or project
- Greater flexibility and freedom as to how work is done, with less supervision
- Working for shorter periods of time, and having a wider variety of work
- Leading you to a full or part-time position as an employee

For more information about contracting, go to **www.guru.com/pro**.

BUSINESS OWNER: You may want to start or buy a business of your own, but be aware that half of start-ups are out of business within 5 years. We recommend you apply principles and practices in this Work Book, and also contact the U.S. Small Business Administration at **www.sba.gov**. If you want to be in business for yourself, but not by yourself, consider buying a franchise. Go to **www.franchise.org**.

VOLUNTEER: There are 2 good reasons to work as a volunteer. You believe in what the organization is doing or really like the work you are doing. If you are starting or changing careers and need experience, volunteering or doing free internships are great ways to learn skills and build contacts. To find organizations in which to volunteer, check opportunities through church, people you know or **www.volunteermatch.org**.

6. Culture: Research shows that matching your values to an employer is the #1 issue in work life. Look for published value statements on employer websites. If you are interested in particular organizations, search the Internet for information about them. Look for people with experience with the employer and ask "what's it really like to work there?" If you completed assessments on career, interests or values, you can compare your results with an employer's culture, work environment and values.

Exercise

Target Opportunities

Work has been prepared for you, and you can find it. Seek to serve others with your gifts, passions and calling. Explore all 6 factors to help you target opportunities from...

- Over 960 major occupations
- More than 100 major industry groups
- Wide range of income levels
- Limitless number of locations
- Four different work platforms
- Variety of organizational cultures

Read and review "How to Target Opportunities" on pages 31-32 and make notes below.

Occupations	Employers

Income _____

Locations _____

Platforms _____

Culture _____

Not all targeting factors may have the same importance to you. For example, Location might be most important to you because you want to move closer to family. Or Occupation and Income might be more important to you than Location or Industry.

Here is your opportunity to prioritize what target factors are most important to you.

RANK MOST IMPORTANT FACTORS 1 THRU 6

Occupations _____   Income _____
Employers _____   Platforms _____
Locations _____   Culture _____

Learn what employers need most

Start by going to websites about your target occupation, industry and employers. Look for information that reveals their needs that match what you do best, such as job postings and descriptions; new growth projects or products; press releases, etc.

What You Do Best	*Employers Need Most*
Experiences	Occupations
Abilities	Employers
Personality	Locations
Interests	Income
Values	Platforms
Spiritual Gifts and Calling	Culture

1. Informational Interviewing

List people you know who work in occupations and industries you targeted. If you can't get an appointment to meet in person, try to talk by phone or trade email. Ask about their jobs, careers and industries. What do they like most and least? What are the opportunities and needs? Are there changes in profession, process and systems? What are typical abilities, talents and skills needed? Ask about other people and resources such as websites, internet news groups, associations and publications. To find more people in target occupations, industries or organizations, you can search through **www.linkedin.com**.

2. Associations

Associations are membership organizations with common interests, such as occupations and industries. Many have meetings, publications, websites and job postings. For over 21,000 association websites, go to **www.asaecenter.org**.

3. Newspapers and Magazines

Professional and trade publications are written for people who work in specific occupations and industries. They are wonderful sources of information on the industry, employers in the industry, key people who work for employers. Go to **www.ipl.org/div/news.**

4. Info and Search Websites

For more info about people, places, anything and everything, start with these 3 websites: **www.google.com**, **www.wikipedia.com**, and **www.about.com**.

Target Your Resumes

The purpose of a resume is to attract an employer to interview and hire you. The 5 key principles to remember are ...

- Be clear about the target opportunity.
- Highlight what you do best that the employer needs most.
- Feature STAR story accomplishments most relevant to the employer.
- Use keywords in job postings that are true of you in your resume.
- Customize each resume for each job.

There are two key parts to writing resumes that get results: Message and Style

Resume Message

The one message that all of resumes should communicate to your target employers is "what I can do for you." Your resumes have about 7 seconds to attract attention to the value you offer. If they like what they see, then they will read more.

Your Best Value Statement

At the top of your resume under your name and contact info, write a HEADLINE with a brief description that connects what you do best with what an employer needs most.

Headlines are 3 to 10 words that highlight occupation and/or industry followed by 3-part description:

Part 1: Employer needs you seek to meet.

Part 2: The experiences, abilities, personality, interests, values, spiritual gift, calling, and/or accomplishment that best meets the employer's needs.

Part 3: The value that employers will receive from the work you do.

Value statement examples that combine headlines with 3-part descriptions:

College CFO Savings & Growth

Seeking an educational organization needing finance, accounting and process improvement. Offering 10 years college CFO experience that achieved growth and substantial savings.

Happy Administrative Help

Looking for a small business needing office management and customer service. Brings administrative abilities and an outgoing personality that improve efficiency and customer satisfaction.

Landscaper Increases Property Looks and Value

Searching for San Diego commercial real estate managers that need landscaping. Providing skills, equipment and attention to detail that will keep the grounds looking great and the value high.

Resumes That Get Results Feature Results

The next most important part of your resume message is featuring accomplishments. Most recruiters, hiring managers and customers believe that the best predictor of future success is past success. Put your most relevant STAR story accomplishments (see page 24) in your resume, describing only the results in as few words as possible. Here is an example:

- Increased sales by 27% in the face of increased competition.

Your objective is to catch the interest of readers so they will want to know how you did what you did.

Basic Resume Components

Contact information: Keep it simple with your name (first-last name), email, phone number at top of page, and your name repeated on the top of second page. Postal address is optional.

Value statements with headline and 3-part descriptions.

Experience and Accomplishments:
- List in reverse historical order for a chronological format.
- Cluster by strengths if you are using a functional resume format.
- Give basic employer/self-employed information such as name, city, dates.
- List positions/title(s) with dates, responsibilities and most especially accomplishments.

Education:
- Show each school, degree, major and accomplishments. Years are optional.
- Omit high school information if you have a college degree.
- List significant extracurricular activities and work while going to school.

Other Sections:
- Professional certifications.
- Work-related technical skills, such as computer proficiencies.
- Community awards (especially significant, work-related awards).

Do NOT include unless relevant to job:
- Personal interests or activities.
- Names of references or the phrase "references available upon request."
- Personal data, such as age, gender, marital status, personal faith.
- Reasons for leaving previous positions.
- Compensation information.
- Photographs.

Message Tips

- Put best value and accomplishments on the top half of the first page.
- Never, ever put anything in your resume that is not completely true.
- Write using short phrases. Use keyword nouns and action verbs.
- Do not use complete sentences or the words "I" or "we."
- Read it again for accuracy. Ask others to read it. Be sure all spelling and punctuation are correct.

To help you stay organized with the rest of the information, we recommend that you complete the "Master Resume" Exercise from which you can write customized resumes. See next page.

Exercise

Master Resume

Think of EVERYTHING you have done, everything you want to promote, everything you did that is "above and beyond." Don't forget info from Work Book exercises on pages 24-25. The more detail you write, the better you can write a customized resume for a job. If you would like to use an expanded Master Resume, go to **www.crossroadscareer.org/masterresume**. Or you can make up your own. Here are the categories of information you should collect.

Your Name _____

Preferred Phone (cell is usually best) _____

Postal Address (optional) _____ City/State/ZIP _____

Preferred Email Address (personal is usually best) _____

Experiences
Most recent employer/self-employment _____ **City/State** _____

Size and description of employer/what they do for whom _____

Position title _____

Dates: From _____ To _____

Major responsibilities _____

Relevant accomplishments _____

Education
Current/Most recent school _____ **City/State** _____

Degree/Major _____ Year _____

Honors/Awards and accomplishments _____

Jobs while attending school _____

Additional Information and Activities
Special talents, knowledge, skills and certifications _____

_____

Talents, interests, skills, personality traits from assessments _____

_____

Job-related interests, hobbies and community service involvements _____

_____

Resume Styles

Resume styles and formats can vary dramatically depending on your target occupations, employers and locations, as well as your career stage and age.

Crossroads Resume Builder - This is a new feature on our website that helps you create a simple, well designed resume which you can print and store online. In order to create your resume via our Resume Builder, register on **www.crossroadscareer.org** as an explorer and click on "Resumes" after you are logged in.

Pongo Resume can help you create top-quality resumes for free:

- **Resume Builder,** with step-by-step instructions and professional layouts.
- **Cover Letter Builder,** with templates and editable, pre-written text.
- **Resume Templates** that are based on your occupation and career goals.
- **24/7 Access** and secure online storage for all your career documents.

You will find that Pongo's free trial can help you find the right resume font and style that fits you best. You also get helpful tips as you create each section of your resume or letter.

For more info, go to **www.pongo.com**

Resume Style Tips
- Keep resume to maximum of two pages. Use minimum of 11-point type.
- Write resumes for people who do not read. They look first before they read.
- Put white space between sections and in margins. Make it visually appealing and easy-to-read.
- Avoid gimmicks, color, fancy borders, boxes, shading or cute graphic designs. Use white paper.
- Get feedback from people who could be good references for you. Make changes as needed.

Resume Online
Tips to maximize opportunity on the web and email for your resume to be picked:

- Best font is 12-point Times New Roman.
- Use Microsoft Word or Adobe PDF.
- Use the built-in resume builder template with a .TXT format of your resume to cut and paste.

- Use nouns or titles instead of verbs, such as "Project Manager" versus "Managed Projects."
- Find keywords in jobs you want – put them in a keyword section at the end of your resume.

There are two basic resume formats:
1. Chronological: Use when you are continuing in the same career path.
   - List work experience in reverse chronological order, listing the most recent experience first.
   - List accomplishments under each employer.
2. Functional: Use when changing, entering or re-entering career.
   - List accomplishments and expertise in functional categories (marketing, sales, etc.).
   - List work experience (company name, job titles, dates).

See basic samples of Chronological and Functional Resumes on the next 2 pages.

Sample of Chronological Resume

Your Name
Your.name@youremail.com
Postal Address or just City, State, Zip
505-555-1234

Write a 3 to 10 word Headline: Clearly targets occupation and employer.

Write your 3-part Strengths and Value Statement ...
Part (1) Target employer needs; **Part (2)** Your experiences, abilities, personality, interests, values, spiritual gifts/calling that meet their needs; **Part (3)** Value that they will receive.

Work Experience

ORGANIZATION NAME
City, State, 20xx-Present

Job Title
- Write 2 or more statements about the work you performed and what you accomplished
- Quantify results of accomplishments and how they contributed to the organization
- Mention on-the-job recognitions and rewards you received that relate to your job objective
- Prioritize statements so the most relevant one comes first

Education

SCHOOL, CITY, STATE
Degree, Major if relevant, Year optional

List scholarships, extracurricular activities, recognitions, rewards and jobs while in school

Other Sections

- Professional certifications
- Job-related technical skills, such as computer proficiencies
- Community or other awards (list only significant, objective-related awards)

Sample of Functional Resume

Your Name
Your.name@youremail.com
Postal Address or City, State, Zip
505-555-1234

Write a 3 to 10 word Headline: Clearly targets occupation and employer.

Write your 3-part Strengths and Value Statement ...
Part (1) Target employer needs; **Part (2)** Your experiences, abilities, personality, interests, values, spiritual gifts/calling that meet their needs; **Part (3)** Value that they will receive.

Professional Accomplishments

KEY STRENGTHS
- Write 2 or more short statements about employment or volunteer accomplishments
- Quantify results of accomplishments and how they contributed to the organization

Work History

ORGANIZATION NAME, City, State, 20xx-Present
Job Title

Education

SCHOOL, City, State
Degree, Major if relevant, Year optional
List scholarships, extracurricular activities, recognitions, rewards and jobs while in school

Other Sections

- Professional certifications
- Job-related technical skills, such as computer proficiencies
- Community or other awards (list only significant, objective-related awards)

Read & Write Devotional

Little White Lies are Big Black Holes

Here is how it works. Almost without thinking, you utter a tiny little lie. Then, when the truth confronts it, tell another lie to protect the first lie. Then the truth comes up again, so you lie again. Soon, you are defending lies with more lies.

What began as a little white lie becomes a big ugly mess. Like big black holes, a pack of lies will suck you into oblivion.

A false witness will not go unpunished, and he who pours out lies will not go free. PROVERBS 19:5

Recheck your resume.
Do any of the words or statements hide one or more little white lies?

If yes, write the lies here.

_____
_____
_____
_____
_____
_____
_____
_____
_____
_____
_____
_____

Then put an X through each and every lie. Forever!

step 5 - searching
Seek to Serve

Rather than just look for a job, seek to serve others with what you do best.

When you search, use both eyes. One eye is for looking according to your plan, and the other eye is for seeing as God directs. Always be prayerful, intentional and alert.

Sometimes finding the right opportunity comes from seeing something you are not seeking. It follows the principle that ...

The mind of man plans his way, but the LORD directs his steps. PROVERBS 16:9 NASB

Start and Grow Your List of Contacts

Make a list of everyone you know: family, friends, neighbors, work associates, past acquaintances, former schoolmates, etc. Search professional associations, publications and research on the Internet to identify potential employers and customers that match your targets for marketing. Informational interviewing is a great way to find more organizations, qualify prospects and list contacts.

Use the "Networking Log" on the next page or a contact management program in your computer. It is important to record who referred who in what organizations so you can contact and follow-up effectively. Get and stay organized every day. Review your progress using SMART goals every week.

Set a minimum goal of making 1 new contact every day. Seek 2 referrals from every contact you make so you can build your list of contacts.

The best strategy combines 3 efforts...

> *All-the-Time Praying*
> **+**
> *On-the-Ground Networking*
> **+**
> *Online Searching*

All-the-Time Praying

Imagine you are dialing 1-800-Dear-God, calling by prayer the one Person who knows everyone, everywhere, all the time. Ask Him every day before every meeting, phone call and email.

He knows the plans He has for you. He knows where all the job openings are. He knows everyone who is hiring. Consider this verse ...

Ask, and it shall be given to you; seek, and you shall find; knock, and it shall be opened to you. MATTHEW 7:7

This might be a good time to spend just 3 minutes scanning again pages 8-9 in this Work Book about hearing and following God's calling. No matter the outcome of the contacts, remember to ...

Be joyful always; pray continually; give thanks in all circumstances, for this is God's will for you in Christ Jesus. 1 THESSALONIANS 5:16-18

Exercise

Networking Log

We recommend you use a computer contact management system like Microsoft Outlook. If you do not have access to a computer or contact management system, you can use this pen and paper version.

Begin by listing as many names as you can of people you know. Make sure to include family, friends, neighbors, former coworkers, people you go to church with, people you play tennis or golf with, parents of your children's friends, former classmates, your lawyer, accountant, financial advisor, dry cleaner, hair dresser, auto mechanic and more. Get phone numbers/email addresses for each one.

Contact Date	Name/Company/Position	Phone/Email Address	Referrals

On-the-Ground Networking

Most employers first try to recruit people through their personal contacts before they advertise a position or post on the Internet. Of all the jobs that get filled, how many are part of this "hidden job market?"

Over 50%

Another startling statistic came from a private corporate study that demonstrated that applicants who had been personally referred were 42 times more likely to be selected than those without personal referrals.

That's a 4,200% better chance!

Why Is This True?

- First, the employer knows someone who knows you.
- Second, you are more likely to be favorably received because of the positive reputation of the referral.
- Third, the likelihood of a match between personal values and corporate culture is higher.

> Amazing, isn't it? Most of the available opportunities are not listed anywhere. It is even truer for contract work and finding customers for your business. You can only find them through personal referrals. That is why we recommend that you spend <u>50% to 85% of your search time networking</u> to make personal contacts, serve others, build relationships, and receive personal referrals.

Plan your networking strategy around several different relationship-building approaches as you seek to:

- Help others with whom you network.
- Find personal referrals to people you wish to reach.
- Join and participate in associations, networking and career groups.
- Get informational interviews about target occupations and employers.
- Ask for opinions on how to best describe your experience and abilities for a particular target opportunity.
- Receive input on your resumes, cover letters, interviews and follow up.

Effective networking starts with helping other people first. Seek to serve and add value to others. It is more blessed to give than receive. If you help enough people get what they want, you will eventually get what you want. Combine a positive attitude, courtesy and flexibility. Say what you will do and do what you say. Be creative, yet thoughtful of each person. For more ideas, see **netweaving.com**.

Four Ways to Connect

1. **In-person** is personal and can be very effective. Meet many people in one place at one time, such as in career fairs, networking events, career groups or association meetings.
2. **Phone** can be both efficient and effective. You can have as many as 5 personal and productive conversations per hour, and follow-up with a brief email.
3. **Email** is very efficient, but not very personal. Email is best for quick introductions and follow-ups, especially if the recipient is expecting your email.
4. **Social networking websites** can be an effective way to be "introduced" one person to another, which can be followed-up by email and phone.

Most of the time you should start with either an email followed by a phone call, or a phone call followed by an email. Your goal is to qualify the person you called as either a potential employer or referral source. Good phone skills are important to engage and make a positive impression.

Making Phone Calls

Calling people about your search can be challenging. It seems even harder when you don't know the people you are calling. Here are some ways to become more effective:

- Practice first with people you know.
- Be in a quiet place with few distractions when you make your phone calls.
- Get permission and use the names of personal referrals.
- Ask your referrals if they will introduce you before you make contact.
- Use a quality landline to call out. Leave your cell phone number for people to call you back.
- Keep your "30-Second Elevator Pitch" script next to the phone.
- Take a break every 30 minutes to stretch and walk around.

Introduce Yourself

Be attentive to what is going on with the person to whom you are talking. If he/she is interested, helpful and positive, keep talking. If he/she is "short" with you and making concluding types of statements, wrap up your conversation. Most calls are 2-10 minutes, unless your contact remains actively engaged.

Here is a Sample Phone Conversation

"Good morning (or afternoon). My name is (give first and last name). *I was referred by* (name of referral)."

Clear the time. *"Do you have a couple of minutes to talk, or would another time be more convenient?"* Do not press to get the time. If later is better for the person you are calling, then ask to book a short phone appointment later. *"When might be a good time for you?"* Always hold conversations with open hands.

Give the reason for your call. *"I am exploring new career opportunities and want to ask you your advice and counsel."*

Ask for the information you want (contacts within a specific company, suggestions on companies that fit certain criteria, advice on how to approach a certain situation, etc.). If you want contacts, you might say, *"I am networking for referrals to* (name of company or people in specific kinds of jobs)." You might also say, *"I am looking for* (give 3 parts of your focus-the job, the industry or company, the location). *Do you know anyone in* (name of company or type of position)?"

Watch your watch! As you see the 10-minute mark coming and going, begin to wrap it up. You might say, *"I want to be thoughtful of your time. May I send you a copy of my resume in case you think of someone or something else later?"* (If yes, get the person's email or postal address.)

Say thank you. *"Thank you for your time and help. It has been a pleasure talking with you."*

Wrap it up. *"If I have an additional question, may I call you back? Thank you and have a great day."*

After a call ...

- Make notes on the conversation as soon as you get off the phone.
- If you are to send an email, note or resume to the person, send it immediately.
- Call or email the referring person with a thank you for the referral.
- Continue to improve your scripts as needed.

Four More Ways to Network

1. Job Support and Networking Groups

Many churches and community service groups have weekly or monthly meetings that offer opportunities to network. Find group meetings on your local daily and business newspaper websites, as well as on **www.crossroadscareer.org**. Be sure to take plenty of your business cards and copies of your resume, as well as your networking list and a notepad.

2. American Job Centers

The U.S. and State Departments of Labor have nearly 3,000 career centers across the country. These centers offer career job postings, transition seminars, career counseling, career fairs and unemployment assistance information. To find locations near you, go to **www.servicelocator.org**.

3. Career and Job Fairs

Look for local opportunities to meet employers and recruiters face-to-face at career and job fairs, usually listed on newspaper, state labor department, and **www.crossroadscareer.org** websites. Some fairs feature a single employer with many openings. Other fairs include multiple employers and are usually focused on a particular occupation, industry, school, community or affinity group.

How to make the most of a fair? Rule number one is to be prepared. Get a list of employers, and know which ones you want to see. First, walk the floor with a map to get an overview. Sort through the employers in which you are interested, and plan a strategy based on how much time you have. Pick up literature from employers that interest you. Avoid getting trapped at any one employer booth and missing others you want to visit. If you are interested, ask if you can make an appointment to talk more in depth.

4. Recruiters

Many employers use recruiting firms to help find and hire candidates. There are 3 types:

1. **Contingency recruiters** are paid by an employer contingent upon the company hiring a person referred by the recruiter. Contingency recruiters usually handle positions that pay less than $100,000/year. Generally they are not the only recruiter trying to fill a position.

2. **Retained recruiters** are paid a retainer by the employer to find candidates for a specific management or specialty position. They handle positions that pay more than $100,000/year and represent these positions exclusively. For a listing of the most established firms, go to **www.bluesteps.com.**

3. **Staffing firms** are also paid by employers, some of which will put you on their payroll and provide benefits as you work on temporary and/or part-time assignments. Go to **www.americanstaffing.net**.

The best method for finding good recruiters is to ask your friends, networking contacts and employers. Select recruiters you trust. Meet them in person if at all possible. Even though recruiters are paid by the employers, you want to work with someone who has *your* best interests at heart.

Be careful of recruiters asking you to sign documents other than reference consent forms, when you are being considered for a specific position. Be sure to read the fine print of any document you might sign. You don't want to be responsible for a placement fee.

Networking Scripts and Cards

Imagine that you are on an elevator. Someone that you know gets on, and asks about how you are doing. You tell them you are seeking a new job/career/work, and they ask, "What are you looking for?" You have less than 30 seconds to respond before the "elevator doors" open and your friend walks off.

Give them a "30-Second Elevator Pitch"
Start the conversation easily, asking about the other person. When the time is right, share your 3-part strengths and value statement you developed for your resume:

- **Part (1)** Employer needs you are seeking to meet
- **Part (2)** Experiences, abilities, personality, interests, values, spiritual gifts/calling
- **Part (3)** The value that employers will receive from the work you do

Sharing the value you offer can take as little as 10 seconds. You have time to answer questions, ask for referrals or a follow-up. Offer your personal card, and ask for his/hers. You can use networking scripts whether you seek traditional employment, work as a contractor or to start a business.

Nervous about speaking to people you don't know well? To learn skills and practice your pitch, find a Toastmasters International group near you at **www.toastmasters.org**.

Go to the next page, and spend at least 30 minutes writing up the "30-Second Elevator Pitch" exercise and calling friends to try it out. Make changes based on what you learn and practice more.

Give them a card: Once you start getting positive feedback, put keywords with your name and contact information on a personal business-size card. Get 250 cards for free at **www.vistaprint.com/free-business-cards.aspx**. Here is a simple example:

Your Name
505-555-1234
Your.Name@Email.com

Accounting, Process Improvement, Leadership
For Schools, Colleges, Universities
Achieve Substantial Savings

Letters and Emails

You need 3 types of emails and letters:

1. An introductory cover letter or email to send your resume
2. Letter or email to request information and contacts
3. Thank you letters and emails to send after interviews

While you can create sample letters and emails in advance, each should be personalized and customized to the particular situation. They should be concise, to the point, appreciative and have 3 parts:

1. The opening sentence should mention a personal referral if you have one and state your objective.
2. The middle part should tell something about you, including 1-2 related accomplishments.
3. The final paragraph includes a call to action, such as "May we talk for a few minutes by phone?"

Exercise

Practice 30-Second Elevator Pitch

Make copies of this exercise sheet for continuous improvement.

Always begin conversations easily. Focus on relationship building and seeking to serve the other person. When the conversation swings around to you, share a brief description of your strengths and value to employer needs using the notes you made on page 34. The description includes 3 parts:

Part (1) Employer needs you are seeking to meet
Part (2) Experiences, abilities, personality, interests, values, spiritual gifts/calling
Part (3) The value that employers will receive from the work you do

---

Example A:

(1) I am seeking an educational organization needing finance, accounting and process improvement. (2) Offering 10 years college CFO experience (3) that achieved growth and substantial savings.

Example B:

(1) I am looking for a small business needing office management and customer service. (2) Bringing administrative abilities and an outgoing personality (3) that improve efficiency and customer satisfaction.

Example C:

(1) I am searching for San Diego commercial real estate managers that need landscaping. (2) Providing skills, equipment and attention to detail (3) that will keep the grounds looking great and the value high.

WRITE your Elevator Pitch using your Strengths and Value Statements. Fill in the blanks below ...

Part (1) Describe the employer needs you are seeking to meet ...

_____

_____

Part (2) List experiences, abilities, personality, interests, values, spiritual gifts/calling that meet needs ...

_____

_____

Part (3) Describe the value that employers will receive from the work you do ...

_____

_____

PRACTICE your Elevator Pitch with friends and family, schoolmates and workmates, especially people you know in/around your target opportunities. Make changes based on what you learn.

Keep improving your Elevator Pitch through practice, practice, practice.

Online Searching

Search online at least 15%, but no more than 50% of your job search time.

Job Boards and Search Engines

Our #1 favorite is the Crossroads Career Job Connection that is a fully integrated into our site **www.crossroadscareer.org/jobs**. Once you register, you get in-network postings of quality jobs, plus your own career dashboard where you can save resumes, cover letters, job searches, plus you get the prayer portal, daily career tips, scriptures and over 200 career and job search resources. **Job posting is free for employers**, as well as Crossroads Career member churches, ministries, colleges, consultants, counselors and coaches.

Our next favorite top 10 *include a variety of leading job and career sites*:

- #1 Site for hourly employment: **www.snagajob.com**.
- Army, Navy, Air Force, Marines, and Coast Guard: **www.usmilitary.com**
- Federal government careers/jobs: **www.usajobs.gov**
- Labor department job banks by state: **www.ajb.dni.us**
- Largest Christian employment site: **www.christianjobwire.com**
- Leading job board for temporary jobs: **www.net-temps.com**
- Local newspapers for jobs and news: **www.50states.com/news**
- Jobs in classifieds on 700 local sites: **www.craigslist.org**
- Search over 8 million job postings: **www.simplyhired.com**
- World's largest marketplace for freelance talent - **www.guru.com**

What about your own business? *Check out these two popular websites:*

1. **www.sba.gov** – U. S. Small Business Administration programs, services, tools, resources and contacts.
2. **www.franchise.org** – International Franchise Association with over 1,250 franchise opportunities.

Search employer websites: This is the best and most direct way to find specific jobs with target employers that match your job search focus. If you see a job posting you want on one of the job posting sites that states the name of the employer, then go right to the employer's website to see if you can find that posting and maybe other job postings of interest. Not only can you get the most complete description of the job and candidate criteria on the employer's website, but you will learn more about the employer, its goals, needs, opportunities and key executives.

Tips for searching online job postings:

- If unemployed, search every day.
- If employed, search every weekend.
- Experiment with keywords/locations.
- Use your networking log and search for jobs with organizations of interest.
- Keep a log of your responses - track website, position, company, date and resume you sent on our dashboard.
- Register for an automatic search agent to notify you of postings in which you are interested.
- When you apply, use keywords that are true of you from the job posting into your resume.
- Start networking for personal referrals from people currently or recently with the target organization.

Connect through Social Networking Sites

Social networks can be a great way to make online connection and bridge to on-the-ground meetings.

Warning! Personal pages on social networking sites will likely be found by recruiters and employers who are considering you for a position. Be careful about the type of information and photos they might find.

Good news! Networking sites can be a great place to plant good information about yourself. Create or modify your member profile that includes what you do best, your value, strengths and accomplishments.

Search for key contacts who are currently or formerly with target employers. While there are thousands of social media sites, start with the two top sites:

1. **www.linkedin.com** operates the world's largest professional network on the Internet with almost 200 million members.
2. **www.facebook.com**: Over one billion active users are connected around the world.

To find people who might help you connect, allow the web's largest job search engine, **www.simplyhired.com**, to confidentially look through your LinkedIn and Facebook contacts.

Get Your Own Email

Your employer may monitor your use of company computers for internet browsing and emailing. Do not use your employer's email address for personal reasons. Get your own email account. Check out these free email services and pick the one that is best for you:

- Gmail from Google: **www.gmail.com**
- Windows: **www.hotmail.com**
- Yahoo! Mail Classic: **www.yahoo.com**

If you already have an email account, change or get a new email address that allows you to use some version of your name, such as john.smith@gmail.com or jsmith@yahoo.com. Do not use a "cute" email. address, such as hotmama@hotpop.com, or nonsensical names or codes.

Here are some suggested tips to use email to your advantage:

- Put your email address in resumes, return email, business cards, letters – everything!
- Put a signature at the bottom of your emails with your name, email and phone.
- If someone refers you to a person whom you are emailing, put that person's name on the subject line.
- When emailing a resume, save it using your name, such as Brenda-Jones-Marketing.doc.
- Confirm appointments by email the day before your meeting or interview.
- After every networking phone conversation, email a thank you.
- Write short emails – ideally with no more than 4 lines.

Post Your Resume Online

Only if your job search is not confidential. If you are employed, and are concerned about your employer finding you searching, then we do not recommend posting your resume on any site. If your search is not confidential, post your resume selectively on the most relevant niche-market or employer sites. Be careful to verify each site. Other tips include:

- Edit your online resumes at least monthly to keep them "active and current."
- Monitor how many hits your resume gets. If you get little or none, try new keywords.
- Do not pay extra to "boost" your resume. Avoid using resume distribution services.
- Do not give any information or fill-out any forms until you verify their credibility.
- Never give your social security or other confidential numbers to anyone.

Read & Write Devotional

And Behind Door Number 3

See, I have placed before you an open door that no one can shut. **REVELATION 3:8**

What open doors do you see right now? Include opportunities to call someone, send a resume, have an interview or accept a work opportunity ...

1.

2.

3.

4.

5.

6.

7.

Opportunity does not necessarily equal God's will. Be careful of open doors!

King Solomon asked for wisdom because he said he was like a little child, not knowing how to go out or come in. Later he wrote…

By wisdom a house is built, and through understanding it is established; through knowledge its rooms are filled with rare and beautiful treasures. PROVERBS 24:3-4

step 6 - sorting
Wow Interviewers

Are you confident that your next interview will result in a job offer?

For most of us, the answer is probably no! Interview success rates average about 10%. How great would it be if your interviewer concluded with "Wow! That was impressive!"

Let's start with 3 basic principles of sorting through opportunities by interviewing and evaluating:

- Help them connect what they need most with what you do best.
- People prefer to hire people they like, so keep generating a positive attitude.
- Interviewing is a 2-way street. Interviewers and employers learn about you. You learn about them.

Next, learn how to wow interviewers and employers. According to Jay Litton, the creator of the **www.wowinterview.com**, it's as simple as PPQ:

- Be the Most **Prepared**
- Be the Most **Passionate**
- And also be **Qualified**

All candidates should meet minimum qualifications, but the biggest difference maker in getting an offer is your being prepared and passionate about the job, employer and opportunity to interview.

Most Prepared and Most Passionate

First, nothing shows preparedness and passion more than creating something especially for the interview, like a written WoW! Interview™ discussion guide. It can be as simple as a single sheet of paper with 4 points:

- The name of the employer, plus your name and the position in which you are interested.
- Why you think the employer is poised for success – positive reasons why the organization is doing well.
- What you can do for the employer – list 3 specific contributions you can make.
- Your career value and goals that match the opportunity the employer is offering.

The second way to demonstrate that you are prepared and passionate is to select STAR stories about your accomplishments that relate to the employer's needs. If you have not written your STAR stories yet, go to page 25 of this Work Book. For each of your accomplishments that illustrate what you can offer, answer these 4 questions:

- What was the Situation you faced?
- What was the Task to be accomplished?
- What were the Actions you took?
- What were the Results you got?

Third, do your homework on the employer as well as the work that needs to be done. Think in advance about what you will say, as well as what you will ask.

On the next few pages, you can prepare for how to wow interviewers by learning:

- 8 types of interviews
- 4 steps to engaging interviews
- How to practice before the interview
- How to prepare for compensation discussion
- How to get ready for testing and referencing

8 Types of Interviews

1. Behavioral Interviews

The interviewer identifies work-related experiences, behaviors, knowledge, skills and abilities that are desirable for a particular assignment. The employer then structures pointed questions to elicit detailed responses aimed at determining if the candidate possesses the desired characteristics. Questions (often not even framed as a question) typically start out: "Tell about a time ..." or "Describe a situation when ..."

Respond with STAR stories most relevant to the question and needs of the employer. Be specific and detailed. Candidates who tell the interviewer about particular situations that relate to each question are more effective. Be prepared with 3-4 STAR stories for each interview.

2. Qualifying or Screening Interviews

These interviews are usually 15 minutes to an hour by telephone. Be prepared with your resume and notes on the employer and position with you. Try to be in a quiet place with no distractions around you. If an interviewer calls without an appointment, ask for few minutes to call back or schedule another time.

Interviewers usually focus on your experience, education, skills, abilities, personality and values. If the interviewer asks about salary, try to delay talk about money until later after you can gain a better understanding of the job and organization. Try to find out more about the job and candidate criteria. Realize that the screening interviewer may not know some of the answers.

3. Hiring Manager Interviews

This interviewer is usually the person to whom you will report if you are hired. They have the most influence on you being hired. When you meet, get to know them, their background and position. Seek to serve them by asking questions about what they want accomplished. Take notes, and be alert for opportunities to connect relationally.

4. Sequential Interviews

It's not unusual to interview with a variety of people in one visit – not only the hiring manager and human resources representative, but also employees in and around the position to be filled. All of them are important! Offer each a copy of your resume. Pay attention to their interests and perspectives, to what needs to be accomplished through the job, and what they say about the hiring manager.

5. Introduction Interviews

The hiring and human resources managers may already have agreed that they want to hire you but need to let senior management get a look. This "chance" meeting is an opportunity to get perspectives from top management on the organization and the work for which you are interviewing.

6. Presentation Interviews

For some jobs and organizations, you may be asked to give a presentation followed by Q&A. The approach is common for sales jobs or organizations. It gives you a chance to show your communication abilities! While you want your presentation to be memorable, avoid using gimmicks or being too cute.

7. Team or Panel Interviews

The advantage is that you have a chance to see how they interact. Address your answers to everyone in the room. Pay attention to the quietest person, who is often the final decision-maker.

8. Stress Interviews

Sometimes interviewers ask difficult questions in hard ways to see how you respond. No matter how frustrating or intimidating, do not lose your cool. Do the best you can, and be firm and friendly.

Gain confidence and learn skills at a local Toastmasters International group: www.toastmasters.org

4 Steps for Engaging Interviews

Consider 4 steps to increase interviewing success: Pray, Prepare, Perform and Praise.

1. Pray

Start with your heart. Fill it with positive thoughts about how to serve the interests of the employer or customer with what you do and like best. Remember, whatever is in your heart will show up on your lips.

The good man out of the good treasure of his heart brings forth what is good; and the evil man out of the evil treasure brings forth what is evil; for his mouth speaks from that which fills his heart. LUKE 6:45 NASB

2. Prepare

Research the employer or customer by visiting their website to read and print information about who they are, what they do, recent news, careers and their jobs. Search the Internet for more information. Call people in your network who may know the organization and people in it. Ask about key issues and trends. Make a list of questions to ask, points to make and STAR stories to share during your interviews.

Work through and practice with a friend the "Interview Before the Interview" Exercises on pages 56-58.

Dress for success. Eat right, exercise, and get plenty of rest the day before the interview. If you need a haircut, get it. If you need new clothing, buy or borrow them. If your clothes need cleaning, do it. Look your best – conservatively. Proper attire varies depending on the organization and the work to be done. Find out what is appropriate in that particular workplace. Read and write the devotional on page 61.

Leave yourself time to get ready. Shower and shave. Wear little or no jewelry, with the exception of a watch, a wedding ring, and (for women) conservative earrings. Do not wear cologne, perfume or other scents. Be sure that your hair is in place and off your face. You want to look professionally well-dressed so the focus will be on what you have to say and not on how you look. Before you leave your home, check yourself in the mirror. Brush and floss your teeth, and take along breath mints.

> **Prepare and take with you a folder with everything you will need for the interview:**
> - Directions to interview location
> - Writing pad and pen for taking notes
> - Extra copies of your resume for each person you will meet
> - Information about the job and employer in a file folder with employer name on the tab
> - List of questions, points you want to make and STAR stories to tell
> - Samples or photos of your work if needed
> - Your WoW! Interview™ discussion guide

Be sure you know the location of the meeting. If you have time, make a test run so you can find the building. Get a map and directions from the Internet. Take money for parking. Get gas the day before, so you do not smell like fuel on interview day. On your way to the interview, think about this key verse ...

Be anxious for nothing, but in everything by prayer and supplication with thanksgiving, let your requests be made known to God. And the peace of God, which surpasses all comprehension, will guard your hearts and your minds in Christ Jesus. PHILIPPIANS 4:6-7 NASB

Arrive at least 15 minutes before your appointment. Avoid doing something stupid in the parking lot, because they might see you. Go to the restroom for one last check; make sure your hair is neat, your clothes are straight, your shoes are clean and your confidence is in place with a smile on your face.

3. Perform

Present yourself to the receptionist at least 5 minutes before the appointment. If offered something to drink, politely decline. Look around for new information on the organization, and be ready to meet the interviewer. Be especially thoughtful of and friendly to people who may not be interviewing you, but will be making observations. While you are waiting, let your mind wander around this verse …

Let no unwholesome word proceed from your mouth, but only such a word as is good for edification according to the need of the moment, so that it will give grace to those who hear. EPHESIANS 4:29 NASB

Greet the interviewer with a warm smile and a firm handshake. Look them in the eyes, and tell them how glad you are to meet them. Look around the office for clues about the person like photos of family, certificates or awards. Ask questions or comment on objects of mutual interest.

When closing the interview, thank the interviewer. Say that you enjoyed the interview and learning about the company. Ask about next steps and timing; take notes on what you find out.

4. Praise

Whether you feel the interview went well or not, praise God from whom all blessings flow. Write thank you notes to the interviewers on nice stationery, as well as send an email. If you are interested in the opportunity, say so. If not, do not. If there is another opportunity in the same organization that appears to be a better fit, ask about it. Whatever the situation, do not burn bridges with anyone.

If you are interested and do not hear back from the employer or customer by the agreed upon date, make a follow-up call and/or send an email to underscore your interest. If you hear nothing back, continue to follow-up once a week for 7 weeks. If you still hear nothing, then let it go.

Keep praying, networking and searching, until you get and accept the offer that's right for you.

The Wow Interview "Rule of Thirds"
Be alert and flexible because the order may vary.

1st Third: Answer the interviewer's questions confidently and honestly. Look for opportunities to share relevant STAR stories. Limit answers to 20 seconds to no more than 2 minutes; the interviewer will ask for more. Feel free to pause to arrange your thoughts; if you do not understand a question, ask for clarification. Always be positive in your answers, and never say anything negative.

2nd Third: As the interviewer describes the job, ask questions about the organization and the person interviewing you, as well as about the work. Seek to understand what needs to be accomplished through the job. You can even ask what they are looking for in the successful candidate – often they will tell you.

3rd Third: When the interviewer asks if you have more questions, respond by saying, "Instead of asking questions, I have created something especially for our meeting today. May I take a moment to share it with you?" When the interviewer says "yes," ask to move closer so that you can point your way through the discussion guide. Before presenting contributions you can make, say "I don't know everything about the position, but I would like to take some risk and share 3 ideas on how to make a positive impact. I would appreciate your feedback." Close by saying, "Because this position meets my top 3 career goals, I want the opportunity to work and contribute."

Wait for their response.

Exercise

Interview Before the Interview, Part 1

The following chart includes some of the most commonly asked interview questions and some tips for answering each one. It's important to use your own words and style when answering questions and to give honest answers.

It is better to have "talking points" in mind rather than trying to memorize answers. Trying to memorize answers creates unnecessary stress for you and may give the appearance that you're not being yourself. For each question, write down some points you would like to make as you answer. Make sure to include work-related accomplishments (STAR stories with situation-task-action-result) whenever appropriate.

Questions	Tips & Talking Points
1. Tell me about yourself.	Because you have done your homework on the interviewer and employers, you can talk about common background and interests, which builds relationship. You can share work-related info such as education, experiences, accomplishments and strengths. Talk no more than 2 minutes.
2. Why do you want to work for us?	Using what you know about the employer and position, focus on their needs and how you can meet them. Emphasize what you do and like best that they need most! Be positive. Convey sense of "I can do it."
3. What do you find most attractive about the position we are discussing?	Talk about the challenges of the position and needs of the employer, and then talk about how your strengths can contribute to the organization's success.
4. What are your strengths?	Give 3-4 work-related strengths. Use STAR stories to give examples of accomplishments and strengths.

Interview Before the Interview, Part 2

Exercise

Questions	Tips & Talking Points
5. Tell me about a time when you achieved your greatest accomplishment.	Use your STAR story to talk about the Situation, Task, Actions and Results. Make it work-related, even related to the position for which you are interviewing. Don't hold back. This is a chance to shine.
6. What are you looking for in salary? What was/is your last/current salary?	Defer this question until later if at all possible. State that you are interested in the overall opportunity to contribute and grow. If you feel you must answer, talk about the total compensation and a salary range.
7. What are your career goals? Where do you want to be in 5 years?	Relate your answer to the position for which you are interviewing. Talk about your desire to grow in your field and to contribute to the organization.
8. Why should we hire you? What contributions can you make?	Give 3-4 strengths supported by examples of accomplishments. Relate them to the needs of this employer/position. Use this opportunity to tell another STAR story.

Exercise

Interview Before the Interview, Part 3

Questions	Tips & Talking Points
9. What are your weaknesses?	Be prepared to talk about a time when you failed to achieve your goals. Keep it brief. Do not elaborate. Tell what you have learned or done to improve.
10. Tell us about a conflict with a boss or co-worker. How was it resolved?	Note that if you say no, some interviewers will keep drilling deeper to find a conflict. The key is how you behaviorally reacted to conflict and what you did to resolve it. A STAR story can work nicely here
11. Why did you leave/are you leaving your last/current position?	If you are employed, talk about your goals and plans for meeting them, seeking new opportunities. Tell them if you were laid off, fired or quit. Share with them what you learned and how it helps you contribute in your next job. DO NOT say anything negative about any past employer or boss.
12. What do you know about our organization?	Do your research. Check the employer's website, and talk to anyone you can find who works there. Include information about the organization's mission, services, products, markets, size, scope.

Prepare for Money Talk

Discussions about wages, salary and benefits do not have to be stressful. They help you qualify the opportunity. Here are some tips:

- Do your homework on similar positions using **www.salary.com**.
- Ask the employer how they have budgeted for the position before or during interviews.
- If you are told the salary, ask if it is the *hiring* range or the *position* range. Most organizations hire at less than the mid-point of the position range so you can earn raises without a promotion.
- If you are asked about desired or current salary, try to delay. If asked on a job application, leave the space blank or write "negotiable." Tell them you like to understand about the position first. If they insist on knowing, give a broad range, but maybe hold back on your absolute minimum.
- Check their website for information on benefits. Ask about benefits after an offer is made.
- Be careful about ruling out an opportunity because it does not pay enough. After they meet you, they may pay more than planned, or they may have another better opportunity for you.
- For more information, go to "Understanding the Offer" exercise on page 64.

Get Ready for References

Referencing is about employers interviewing others who know about you.

Be ready to provide reference contacts when asked. Reference requests are most appropriate after interviews have established a mutual interest between you and the employer or customer. Ask with whom they would like to speak. Have a master list of references already prepared so you can select the people best suited for a particular opportunity. Call or email people to ask them to be a reference. Prepare them for who will be calling.

Complete the "Master Reference List" exercise on the next page.

Remember that referencing is a 2-way street, too. You are evaluating them while they evaluate you.

Ask the employer for references, such as people who currently or used to work in the department, as well as customers and vendors. Call people you know in or around the organization.

Ask references about their experience with the organization. Assure them of confidentiality, that is you will not report what they say. Be specific in asking questions about not only the organization and work to be done, but also the people. Ask about culture and operation values. Sample questions include ...

- What are the critical issues the organization faces? How do/did you like working there?
- What can you tell me about the work to be done and others who have worked in the job?
- How would you describe the boss and others around the position – strengths and struggles?

Plan for Testing

Testing is a common tool employers use to assess if you have the skills or personality to fit the position. Being asked to take a test is good because it suggests that hiring the right person is important to them.

The key to taking tests is the same as interviewing – eat right, exercise and get plenty of rest. You want to be energetic and relaxed. Be honest with your answers because it is all about fit. If you have taken assessments that show you to be a good fit, offer to share the results.

If the testing shows that your skills or personality do not fit the position, consider that as good news. You do not want to be in a position or organization that is not a fit for you.

Exercise

Master Reference List

Make a list of everyone who could/should be a reference for you, then pick the best 2-5 most relevant references for a specific opportunity you are considering. Ask permission from each reference before giving their name. It is even better to send them a copy of your resume so they can give you feedback, as well as be prepared to act as a reference.

For each reference, list the name with the one they are normally addressed, nature of your personal or professional relationships, their email address, preferred phone number and special notes. Be sure to check spelling of their name and accuracy of contact information.

Name	Relationship	Email	Phone	Notes
Edward Example	Mgr., ABC Company	Edward@abc.com	555.123.4567	Edward left ABC; now director at XYZ
Sam Sample	Personal Friend	Sample@church.com	444.123.4567	Director of mission agency where I volunteered

Read & Write Devotional

Dress for Success

Put on the full armor of God so that you can take your stand against the devil's schemes ... Stand firm then, with the belt of truth buckled around your waist, with the breastplate of righteousness in place, and with your feet fitted with the readiness that comes from the gospel of peace. In addition to all this, take up the shield of faith, with which you can extinguish all the flaming arrows of the evil one. Take the helmet of salvation and the sword of the Spirit, which is the word of God. EPHESIANS 6:11; 14-17

Draw a picture of yourself wearing the full armor of God. Here are the items:

1. Belt
girded with truth

2. Breastplate
of righteousness

3. Shoes
gospel of peace

4. Shield
of faith

5. Helmet
of salvation

6. Sword
Word of God

How will the armor of God help you to *stand firm*? _____

_____

Spiritual "underwear" is more important than physical outerwear. Post this devotional where you will see it while you dress. The full armor of God ... don't leave home without it!

step 7 - selecting
Walk in Good Works

Luck is when opportunity meets someone who is prepared.

Let's review the foundational principle of walking through a crossroads in your career ...

[You] are His workmanship, created in Christ Jesus for good works, which God prepared beforehand so that [you] would walk in them.
EPHESIANS 2:10 NASB

As you search and sort for opportunities, remember that looking for work is work. Keep seeking and seeing what God has prepared — not only the promise of a future and a hope, but the process of selecting. Be alert as you pray for His vision, wisdom and strength.

Get Offers - Make Offers

In the new world of work, you do not just wait for offers, you make offers. Let's say you see an opportunity you believe is right for you. In your mind, you have already selected it, even though there is no offer to accept.

Think "ME, Inc." Consider yourself a 1-person corporation owned by God. No matter who you seek and what they want, identify needs and propose solutions. Figure out what they want accomplished, and recommend how they can get the results they want.

Be open to being hired as an employee, a self-employed contractor or a business owner providing a service. Be open about compensation, too. Even when there is no money to be paid, you can barter for food, clothing and shelter.

To Get an Offer

1. Follow-up every week for 7 weeks with the decision-maker by either email, phone call or letter.
2. Every week, demonstrate that you are the most prepared, most passionate and also qualified.
3. Each week check the news and their website to feature a different message about what they need most that you do best.
4. Search for other opportunities in case this one goes away.
5. If you get an offer from a second employer, tell the first employer.
6. Make an offer.

To Make an Offer

1. Write a one-page proposal with five parts: their needs, your services, time, results and money.
2. Describe their needs as described in job posting and/or the interview.
3. Describe the services you provide that meets their needs.
4. Outline a recommended work plan, timeline and estimated cost.
5. Describe the results they can expect.
6. Seek to talk the proposal through with them, make changes, then send a final written proposal.

How to Evaluate Offers

If an offer is made, listen attentively and respectfully. Take notes and repeat to verify the offer. If you are not clear about any aspect of the offer, ask questions. If it is a professional or salaried position, ask for the offer to be put in writing and sent to you. Do not immediately debate or negotiate. Do not accept or decline. Tell them how appreciative and interested you are. Ask when an answer is needed.

If you receive a written offer, review it carefully. Make notes of questions. If you are not good with details, ask a trusted family member or friend to review the written offer. Call or email the key contact person with questions. If you have concerns or you need to negotiate, seek to meet them in-person.

How to know whether a particular opportunity is really God's calling:

- Compare the opportunity with what you learned in Steps 1 through 4.
- Take time away alone to think, and time with your spouse if you are married.
- Talk through your decision with trusted advisors, including family members and close friends.
- If your doubts persist, talk through your concerns with the potential employer.
- If you do not feel peace inside about the decision, do not accept the offer.
- Review how to "Hear and Follow God's Calling" on pages 8-9.
- Do what you believe God wants you to do.

Selecting an opportunity should be based on a win-win approach; you should be focusing on selecting the right opportunity both for you and your future employer or customer. Think in terms of collaboration instead of a compromise. Some points to consider are:

- Know in advance what is important to you based on your needs, wants and values.
- Assess the needs of the employer in terms of the results to be achieved and rewarded.

A job is not just what you do 8 hours (or more) a day; a job involves the organization, other employees, a boss and so much more. Getting to know the full scope of the opportunity takes work. So let's get started!

- Understand the title, the reporting relationships, the hours of work per week, the amount of travel.
- Find out details such as the expected dress code, working hours and if telecommuting is available.
- Get a feel for the culture, especially the personalities and values of the key players.

Understand the employment offer by asking these questions:

- What is the starting salary? What is the total salary range for the position? Is the offer flexible?
- How often are performance and salary reviewed?
- Is there commission or bonus? How much is it? What is it based on? When is it paid?
- Is there a hiring bonus? Ask about reimbursement for lost bonus from current employer.
- Is there use of a car or is there a car allowance?
- Is equity in the company available in the form of stock or options?
- What about 401(k) and savings plans?
- Is there insurance (health, dental, life, disability, other)?
- Are there deferred compensation plans, savings plans, etc.?
- If relocation is required, what is covered? The move? House sale? Temporary living? Commuting?

Make copies of and complete the exercises on the next 3 pages:

- Understand the Offer
- Decision-Making
- Win-Win Negotiation

Exercise

Understand the Offer
Make copies of this form.

This worksheet is another tool for evaluating offers when they come. Complete it now so that you can be objective about what's important to you. Then make copies to use for evaluating each offer you receive.

Name of potential employer	Name of hiring manager
Positives about opportunity	Concerns and Questions
How much the company seems to want you	How much you want the company

Cash Compensation	Last Year	This Year	Next Year	Want	Need
Base Salary					
Bonus					
Commission/Other $					
Total Cash Compensation					
Other: Car, Stock Options, Club Membership, Equity					
Total Other Cash Value					
GRAND TOTAL CASH					

Benefits	Priority A/B/C	Benefits	Priority A/B/C
Weeks of Vacation		Home Office	
Health Insurance		Family Medical Insurance, Co-Pay?	
Dental Insurance		Paid Holidays	
Vision Insurance		Sick Days	
Life Insurance		Retirement/401K/Matching/Pension	
Long-Term/Short-Term Disability		Deferred Compensation	
Employee Assistance Program		Tuition Reimbursement	
Training		Overtime	
Severance Agreement		Relocation	
Tech Support		Help with Spouse's Employment	
Day Care for Children		Temporary Living Expenses	

Other Factors		Other Factors	
Title		Flexible Hours	
Hours per Week		Free Time	
Travel % (nights away)		Team vs. Individual Work	
Promotability		Entrepreneurial	
Management Experience/Training		Location	
High- vs. Low-Risk Opportunity		Cost of Living Index Comparison	

©1999-2012 Westerberg & Associates – Used by permission

Exercise

Decision-Making
Make copies of this form.

Use this worksheet when you get a job offer so you can compare the criteria of what you believe God has prepared for you with the opportunity being offered to you. Make copies of the worksheet for evaluating opportunities as you receive them.

_____ with _____
       (Work Opportunity)   *(Organization)*

Criteria Desired	**Work Opportunity**
Work function	**Work function**
Employers	**Employers**
Location	**Location**
Salary	**Salary**
Other Compensation/Benefits	**Other Compensation/Benefits**
Abilities	**Abilities**
Interests	**Interests**
Personality	**Personality**
Values	**Values**
Other Criteria: 1. 2. 3.	**Other Criteria:** 1. 2. 3.

Exercise

Win-Win Negotiation
Make copies of this form.

Strategy
- Not - they win, you lose
- Not - you win, they lose
- Not - compromise, each gets half
- But - collaborate for a win-win

Steps
- Establish your value first
- Highlight results from what you do best
- Know what you need in money, benefits and more
- Do your homework at **www.salary.com**
- Negotiate mutual interests and not positions
- Focus on WE and not just ME

1. **Fully understand an offer before you begin negotiating.** In addition to salary, understand all the benefits, performance review process, and so much more. Write down any questions you need to ask so you can fully understand the offer.

2. **Know what you are willing to give up and what you are not.** List the things you are *not* willing to give up. Be honest!

3. **Try to anticipate what the potential employer is not willing to give up.** List them.

4. **Negotiate the small things first.** Items such as additional vacation, flex time or working from home a few days a week may be small things to the employer but big things to you. Negotiate them first; then move to the big things, like salary. Determine now what small things you will use in the beginning of your negotiations.

Remember:
Collaborate so both parties give up some things that are *not* so important to them, so that both parties feel that they are WINNERS!

Not It

How frustrating to be at Step 7 and the offer does not work – you feel you are instantly back to the beginning.

It not only can happen, but it will happen. One of our ministry leader volunteers was looking for his next job after being laid-off. On a particularly wonderful Friday, he had 10 opportunities developing, 3 of which looked like they would bring offers the next week. By noon the next Monday, all 10 were gone! He took a deep breath, learned from this amazing experience and started over. His next job was so good that after a few years, it allowed him to retire.

The most important thing is what you do next. Here are some suggestions:

- Explore with the employer whether "No" really means "No." Are there ways to collaboratively re-engage with the hiring manager or HR representative?
- Might there be other jobs with the employer now or in the future that might be a better fit?
- Respond to a "no" offer or decline an offer with grace. Also keep an eye on keeping the relationships. The job you don't get or take now might well be the way to land a better job later with the same employer.
- Remember that some of the best decisions end with the word "No!" Either you or the employer or both of you had "good reasons." If it is a door God has closed, then say "thank you."
- Learn from your experience. What could you have done better or differently? See if you can get feedback on your interview. In baseball, a good batting average is 300, which means 7 of 10 times the batter was out. Analyze your pitch and swing, and get up to bat again.
- In the future, always try to have 2 more opportunities developing at the same time. It builds confidence, makes you more secure in negotiations and provides an immediate alternative.
- Review "Reach Forward" on page 18 to regenerate a positive attitude.
- Review "Hear and Follow God's Calling" on pages 8-9.

Got It

Accept the final offer only if you believe it is work prepared for you, have received counsel and confirmation from your close advisors and have reached consensus with your spouse. Be sure you get the offer in writing, and find out when you need to give an answer. But remember, this isn't the end of the process!

You are starting a new job or career. Many people, having gotten this far in the process, think they are finished. They breathe a sigh of relief and relax. Not a good idea.

Getting a *good start* in a new job is the most important step of this walk, not just getting the job. More than one new job has come unraveled after the start date. To help you get going on the right foot:

- During your first months at the job, arrive early and stay late.
- Ask lots of questions. Take many notes.
- Review your notes and progress with your boss every week.
- Get a feel for who does what and what each person is like.
- Observe organizational politics, but do not participate.

For more new job tips, download a copy of the "New Job Jump Start" e-booklet at **www.crossroadscareer.org/newjob**.

Prepare for Your Next Move

"What? I just got here!" you say. The last thing you want to think about is another job search!

In this new world of work, temporary, part-time and contract work is part of the mix of jobs available. Since you are responsible for your own career – from planning to job search – it is wise to stay alert and active every week. With the speed of change combined with the economic destruction and construction of whole occupations, industries and even communities, you need to be prepared.

Here are suggested steps that might help:

- Be flexible and focus on serving others.
- Look for opportunities to do extra assignments and get extra education.
- Continue to update your master resume and your references at all times.
- Keep networking to expand your contacts for upcoming assignments
- Seek purpose in your work.
- Exercise your values at work.
- See your work as ministry.
- Approach each day as an opportunity to write a new STAR story.

Learn that the secret to job success is actually in the word JOB:

- **J** for joy in your job.
- **O** for obedience.
- **B** for doing your best.

Be a good steward of whatever God gives you. Don't worry about what He doesn't give you because you have no responsibility for what He does not give you. Remember that you are God's workmanship, created in Christ Jesus for good works that God prepared beforehand for you to walk in them.

So stay alert and keep on the path through crossroads that God prepared for you, so that you can find life just as Jesus promised ...

I came that they might have life, and might have it abundantly.
JOHN 10:10 NASB

Pass it Forward

In today's ever-changing world of work, you want to keep all bridges open and all fences mended. Take time to do these important activities once you have started your new job:

- Write a thank-you note to everyone who helped you along the way. Let them know the name of your new employer, your new title and/or position, your new work phone number and your new email. Tell them how they helped you in the midst of this career crossing.
- Be ready, willing and able to help other people through crossroads in their careers. You of all people know what a roller coaster ride it is to go through a career transition. Actively think about how you can help others with contacts, counsel and encouragement.
- Share with them the 7 steps to maximize their careers by hearing and following God's calling.

... that we will be able to comfort those who are in any affliction with the comfort with which we ourselves are comforted by God.
2 CORINTHIANS 1:4 NASB

Congratulations
This Amazing Race Continues!

Congratulations on completing the work in this Work Book. Take a break, celebrate and get back out there!

May we suggest rewarding yourself (and your mentor or group) with a celebration of fellowship around a meal next week?

You may or may not have found a new job or career yet, but hopefully you have made progress and begun maximizing your career potential – being more faithful with where you are, as you prepare for what's next. Perhaps you continue with your group – or perhaps start or join a new one?

Take Your Choice of Tracks

…let us also lay aside every encumbrance and the sin which so easily entangles us, and let us run with endurance the race that is set before us… Hebrews 12:1 NASB

Go through the Work Book again…
- Perhaps you join another workshop or class just starting
- Maybe you help facilitate or lead
- Be a mentor to someone else

Continue with your group for fellowship and support…
- Use the C3G (Christ-Centered Career Group) meeting plan
- Provides practical, personal, spiritual support in the unemployment journey
- Does not require a study curriculum

Consider 1 of the 3 studies already prepared for you in www.crossroadscareer.org.
- *"Real Success at Work: Hearing and Following God's Calling"*: a 4-week individual or small group study on calling.
- *"What the Bible Says to You If You Are Between Jobs"*: a 10-chapter, 41-page exploration of principles and truths learned through job loss.
- *"New Job Jump Start: 30 Days with over 100 Ways to Get a Great Start in Your New Job"*: a 4-week individual or group study on starting a new job or restarting an old one

Help us to help others find jobs, careers and God's calling:
- Refer friends, family and others to **www.crossroadscareer.org**
- Join or start a Crossroads Career ministry. See **www.crossroadscareer.org/groups**
- Support financially, so we can help more people at **www.crossroadscareer.org/donate.**

Join the movement! With 150 million people in America at crossroads in their careers, there is need and opportunity to help everyone find jobs, careers and God's calling. Crossroads Career Services, Inc., is an IRS approved 501c3 public charity that provides resources for churches, ministries, colleges, consultants, counselors and coaches.

1-800-Dear-God

For the journey ahead

The Heavenly Blue Pages

When in sorrow	call John 14
When you have sinned	call Psalm 51
When you worry	call Matthew 6:19-34
When you are in danger	call Psalm 91
When God seems far away	call Psalm 139
When your faith needs stirring	call Hebrews 11
When you are lonely and fearful	call Psalm 23
When you grow bitter and critical	call I Corinthians 13
When you feel down and out	call Romans 8:31
When you want peace and rest	call Matthew 11:25-30
When the world seems bigger than God	call Psalm 90
When you want Christian assurance	call Romans 8:1-30
When you leave home for labor or travel	call Psalm 121
When your prayers grow narrow or selfish	call Psalm 67
When you want courage for a task	call Joshua 1
When you think of investments and returns	call Mark 10
If you are depressed	call Psalm 27
If your pocketbook is empty	call Psalm 37
If you are losing confidence in people	call I Corinthians 13
If people seem unkind	call John 15
If discouraged about your work	call Psalm 126
If self pride/greatness takes hold	call Psalm 19
If you want to be fruitful	call John 15
For understanding of Christianity	call II Corinthians 5:15-19
For a great invention/opportunity	call Isaiah 55
For how to get along with fellow men	call Romans 12
For Paul's secret to happiness	call Colossians 3:12-17

Alternate Numbers:

For dealing with fear	call Psalm 34:7
For security	call Psalm 121:3
For assurance	call Mark 8:35
For reassurance	call Psalm 145:18

Emergency numbers may be dialed direct. No operator assistance is necessary. All lines to Heaven are open 24 hours a day!

Or post a prayer at **crossroadscareer.org**

Author, Acknowledgements and Permissions

Author Brian Ray is founder of the Crossroads Career Network. Formerly, he was VP for Human Resources and Administration for the Chick-fil-A restaurants chain. Brian also owns Primus Consulting, an executive leadership search and consulting firm.

Brian is a graduate of the University of North Carolina at Chapel Hill with BA in Journalism and the University of Illinois with MS in Communications. Brian and his wife, Kristy, reside in Charlotte, North Carolina and are members of Transformation Church.

More than 100 executives and experts in human resources, recruiting, career coaching, job search, resume writing, training and development contributed to this Work Book and its online resources.

All scripture quotations, unless otherwise indicated, are taken from the Holy Bible, New International Version®, NIV®. Copyright ©1973, 1978, 1984, 2011 by Biblica, Inc. Scripture quotations taken from the New American Standard Bible® Copyright © 1960, 1962, 1963, 1968, 1971, 1972, 1973, 1975, 1977, 1995 by The Lockman Foundation at www.Lockman.org

---

Page 4 'The Coming Jobs War" By Jim Clifton Copyright ©2011 Gallup Press, Page 102

Page 4 "Face to Face Volume One: Praying the Scriptures for Intimate Worship" by Ken Boa, Zondervan Publishing House Copyright ©1997. Introduction Page X

Page 5 "Workers Less Miserable, but Hardly Happy" June 12, 2012 Press Release from Conference Board at **www.conference-board.org**

Page 5 "16 Tons" originally sung my Merle Travis at Capitol Studios, Hollywood, CA, Aug 8, 1946, released as Capitol Recording 48001 in 1947

Page 6 "Half in U.S. Don't Use Their Strengths Throughout the Day" September 12, 2012 article on **www.Gallup.com** by Dan Witters, Jim Asplund, and Jim Harter.

Page 10 Definition of "career" from **www.Dictionary.com**

Page 10 Definition of calling comes from Greek word Kaleo in "Vine's Expository Dictionary of New Testament Words" at **www2.mf.no/bibel/vines.html**

Page 15 "Over The Top" by Zig Ziglar Copyright ©1994 The Zig Ziglar Corporation. page 127

Page 17 "The Bondage Breaker" Copyright ©1990 Neil T. Anderson page 196

Page 19 "Freedom From Fear" Copyright ©1999 Neil T. Anderson and Rich Miller

Page 21 "Wellbeing" by Tom Rath and Jim Harter Copyright @2010 Gallup Press

Page 22 "If It Ain't Broke, Break It! And Other Unconventional Wisdom for a Changing Business World," Copyright© 1992 Robert J. Kriegel. Page 259

Page 30 "Face to Face Volume One: Praying the Scriptures for Intimate Worship" by Ken Boa, Zondervan Publishing House Copyright© 1997. Introduction Page X

Page 52, 54, 55 All references to the Wow Interview™ are Copyright© 2011 by The Litton Group. See **www.wowinterview.com**.

Page 64 "Understand the Offer" by Jeff Westerberg. Copyright© 2012 Westerberg & Associates.

MORE HELPFUL RESOURCES

for your "next steps" visit www.crossroadscareer.org/store

Getting a New Job

Getting a new job and getting a great start at that job are two different things. You want to have every possible advantage for success in your career. This is one of those great advantages--30 days with over 100 ways to get a great start in your new job.

Real Sucess at Work

Imagine getting up every day with the conviction that you are on the planet for a purpose. How fulfilled and fruitful would you be to know that you and your work matter to God and that He is pleased? How great would it be to experience real success? This study of Ephesians 2:10 helps you to discover how to hear and follow God's calling

English-Spanish Work Book

Escrito para las personas en cada fase de su carrera, de los graduados de la escuela secundaria a los jubilados, este Libro de Trabajo de Carrera ® Work (70 páginas) incluye la enseñanza bíblica, los ejercicios prácticos y los devocionales – todos diseñados para ayudarle a escuchar y seguir el llamado de Dios. Cubre temas prácticos, como la evaluación y oportunidades dirigidas, así como hojas de vida, creación de redes, la búsqueda en línea yentrevistas